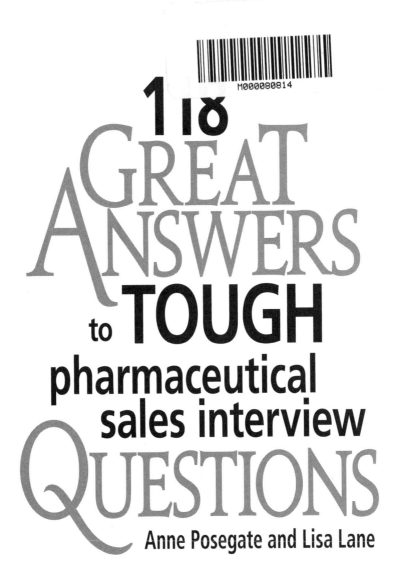

118
A GREAT ANSWERS
to **TOUGH**
pharmaceutical
sales interview
QUESTIONS

Anne Posegate and Lisa Lane

Drug Careers, Inc.
Clarksburg, NJ.

118 Great Answers to Tough Pharmaceutical Sales Interview Questions
by Anne Posegate and Lisa Lane

Copyright © 2009 Drug Careers Inc.

Published by Drug Careers, Inc.
P.O. Box 543
Clarksburg NJ 08510

ISBN: 978-0-9717785-6-6

Cover and interior design by 1106 Design

Printed in the United States of America

DEDICATION

To my husband, Bret Posegate: Your encouragement and confidence in me has made this book possible. I love you!

To my parents, Tom and Viola Barnard: You taught me the importance of prayer and determination, and instilled in me a strong work ethic. I'm so proud to be your daughter.

—AP

This book is dedicated to my husband, Jeff and my children, Lauren and Jake.

Jeff, you have always supported me in all that I do. Your "go for it" advice has made all of this possible. You're the best!

Lauren and Jake, you two are the reason that I do what I do! You make every day fun, and you mean the world to me.

—LL

TABLE OF CONTENTS

One important key to success is self confidence. An important key to self confidence is preparation.

—*Arthur Ashe*

INTRODUCTION TO 118 GREAT ANSWERS TO TOUGH PHARMACEUTICAL SALES INTERVIEW QUESTIONS

We leave no stone unturned as we pose 118 questions that are routinely asked in *real* pharmaceutical sales interviews. This is your inside track—it's almost like cheating on a test. Armed with the information in this book, you will already know the questions before you step into the interview chair! We don't really think of this as cheating. Rather, we like to call it "working smart."

You now have a huge edge over other candidates. As you read on, not only will you learn what to expect, you will also gain valuable insight into the world of pharmaceutical sales. Study these questions and learn how to give "knock-their-socks-off" answers. Your goal is to land that dream job in pharmaceutical sales. This book will help you achieve your goal. Go ahead ... close your eyes and imagine yourself with that commission check in hand. If you like what you envision, read on!

This book gives you access to the most commonly asked questions—but don't just read the questions. Take the time to fill in the responses with your own answers, and practice with a partner. Next ... practice, practice, practice! Why? It's simple—if you've rehearsed your answers until your delivery is smooth, you'll be able to focus on the interviewer and read his or her body language. These nonverbal cues will provide you with insight as to how well the interview is progressing and will also give you hints as to whether your answers are hitting your interviewer's hot buttons. When you are well prepared, it will show. Not having to worry about your answers will allow you to focus on the other factors that contribute to a successful interview. You will be more relaxed and able to let your true personality show. You will find yourself in the "interviewing zone", meaning that you can go into the interview with confidence, fully prepared to eliminate your competition. Why? Because you will have adequately prepared in a way that 99.9 percent of candidates are unwilling to do.

Pharmaceutical sales is one of the most sought-after careers in the United States. The competition is fierce. If you have landed an interview, you have what it takes on paper; but that alone isn't enough. Your résumé may have gotten noticed and may have been pulled from those of over 500 applicants, but you may still be one of 30 or so candidates going for one opening. In that case, it's show time. Show your potential employers that you have done your homework, that you want to work for them, and that you have what it takes to be a successful pharmaceutical sales rep. This book is designed to help you do just that.

Put your thinking cap on

Before you delve into the actual interview questions and answers, it's important to think about what pharmaceutical sales managers will be looking for in a great sales rep. What type of person do they want to add to their team? Your answers to their interview questions need to show them that you are the perfect fit for the job. Here's what they will be looking for in the ideal rep:

- **Communication skills.** Show them that you are adept in both verbal and nonverbal communication skills, that you are an exceptional listener, and that you are willing to work to understand the physician and his or her needs. Prove that you are an excellent rapport builder and that you have the ability to connect with others to build friendships and alliances.

- **Organization skills.** Convince them that you keep good records of activities performed. Demonstrate that you know how to prioritize and plan for the next day by knowing which physicians you'll see and what incremental goal you'll focus on with each of them. Tell them that you are flexible enough to take advantage of opportunities when they arise and that you have the ability to prioritize and to make the most of your opportunities.

- **Openness to guidance and constructive criticism as an opportunity to learn.** Convince them that you are coachable and are eager to listen to helpful advice.

- **Loyalty.** You will stand by your company despite issues and never speak critically about the company.

- **Ability to take ownership of territory.** You will view your territory as your own business and provide leadership to others when necessary.

- **Problem solver/opportunity creator.** You can help your physician solve his or her patient problems and address patient needs.

- **Good negotiation and persuasive selling skills.** You can anticipate prescriber's customers needs and wants through questioning techniques, rapport building, and patient population analysis. You provide exceptional customer service and act as a partner in serving the physician's patients.

- **Ability to present information in a clear, concise manner.** Demonstrate proving your assertions through "show and tell" and effective application of analogies and comparisons.
- **Ability to memorize and comprehend large amounts of technical scientific and medical information.**
- **Determination and competitive attitude.** You will work extra hours as needed and focus on goals until you achieve them. You have a drive to succeed and be the best. You exhibit a "get what you put into it" mentality in terms of time, energy, and effort.
- **Teamwork skills.** Demonstrate your ability to work toward a common goal and to motivate and inspire others.
- **Positive, enthusiastic attitude.** You'll maintain a positive attitude no matter what and despite setbacks.
- **Professional appearance and conduct.** You will represent the company well.
- **Confidence and motivation to be a self-starter.** You do not wait for others to teach you what you need to know. Your "whatever it takes" attitude is obvious.

STAR Answer Format
(to help you wow your interviewer!)

If you really want to impress, develop a STAR response for every bulleted skill or quality listed above. This will enable you to prove during the interview that you possess those skills or qualities. STAR is always a good answer format to use, but it is particularly effective when answering situational questions.

Here's how to answer effectively in STAR format:

S = **Situation** (State the situation you were in.)

T = **Task** (Explain the task you needed to complete.)

A = **Action** (Talk about the action you took.)

R = **Result** (Recount the results of your actions.)

Rules to answer by

(Keep these important rules in the back of your mind as you answer each question during an interview.)

- Always back your answer up with personal, real-life examples.
- Don't just say, "I can do this and I can do that." For every skill you mention, recall an incident when you successfully applied that skill.
- Don't just say, "Yes I can!" Explain how you will do it and why you will be good at it.
- Your answers to interview questions should always answer the question, "But how?" For example, don't just say, "Yes, I absolutely can increase sales! I just know that I have what it takes to make it in this business!"
- Show them how you can do it.

NOW ... on to the Index of
Pharmaceutical Sales Interview Questions!

Before we begin...

Before we get into the categorized questions, let's talk about a very important question—the question you will more than likely be asked *first* when you walk into an interview, the question that sets the tone for the interview and allows you to make or break your first impression. Let's call it "Question 1A." *(It's probably the most important question you can answer, so pay close attention and practice a great answer!)*

 Tell me about yourself. *(You must be able to answer this one. It's a definite!)*

What They're Really Trying to Determine: Your interviewers want to know if you will make an appropriate addition to their team. You will need to show that you are a leader, achiever, and extrovert with a history of successes. The bottom line is that they want to know if you have what it takes to succeed in pharmaceutical sales. They want to see what type of person you are, and they are looking for personality with this answer.

What Not to Do: Don't ramble and talk about too many details or talk about a time in your life that the interviewer could care less about.

Your Plan/Great Answer: The best way to begin is to ask them where they would like you to begin. If they are interested only in information about your time with your current employer, why start out talking about college? Once you find out where to begin, make a short, organized statement of your achievements and goals. Give a brief overview of your résumé. As you talk about your skills and achievements, relate their relevance to a successful pharmaceutical sales career.

Your Response: _____

_____

_____

_____

_____

Section 1
Teamwork

If you have done your research about how most pharma sales forces are structured, you know that as a rep, you are always part of a team. Managers will be looking to hire individuals who can get along well as a part of the sales district and, if necessary, as a part of a team that sells together to meet territory goals. Your goal in answering these questions is to prove that you will make an excellent addition to the team.

What is "teamwork"?
Teamwork involves the following:

- Team members understand, support, and defend each other's actions.
- Team members commit to a team goal that overrides individual goals.
- Individual efforts create synergy; that is, the results of the team are greater than the sum of the parts.
- Team members help develop other team members.

- Team members accept accountability, taking ownership of success or defeat.
- Team members try to learn and improve, continually developing themselves.
- Team members have specific roles.
- Team members provide support and encouragement to each other.

Interview questions and GREAT answers that showcase your Teamwork Beliefs and Abilities

 Have you ever had to make up for the shortcomings of an incompetent boss? Why, and what did you do?

What They're Really Trying to Determine: Are you a team player? Are you loyal?

What Not to Do: Never say anything negative about past managers or companies you've worked with. No matter how right you may be, this is not the time for such discussion.

Your Plan: Even if you've had 20 horrible managers, focus on one manager from whom you learned something positive. Also, try to correlate the skill you learned with a skill required in pharmaceutical sales. Finally, focus on a result of having learned that specific skill.

Great Answer: "I've had the great fortune of working for a number of gifted managers. For example, one manager was especially adept in helping me understand the importance of prioritizing and organization (key requirements of pharma sales jobs). Because my job was so fast-paced, I needed an organization system for prioritizing my key customers and following through on the goals I had set for each client (hmmm … sounds similar to those used in pharma sales). This manager opened my eyes to the lasting benefits of following a plan, prioritizing, and diligently recording customer data. As a result, my sales increased by 67 percent in the three months following my implementation of her organization system."

Your Response: _____

_____

_____

_____

_____

2. **What is more important to you, being a team player or thriving on competition and winning? Do you prefer to work individually or as part of a team?**

What They're Really Trying to Determine: How much of a team player are you? Are you so interested in winning that you'll run over your teammates to do so? If so, they'll want to weed you out right away because such an attitude simply will not make for a cohesive team. Managers know that competitiveness is part of being a good salesperson, especially since reps are ranked, recognized, and rewarded individually. But teamwork is also an important aspect of the job.

What Not to Do: Saying that you have to win at all costs and that it doesn't matter whose toes you have to step on is a bad, bad move. Appearing overly competitive and aggressive will not win you the job.

Your Plan: Show your understanding that you need both a competitive spirit and teamwork mentality to succeed in pharmaceutical sales jobs.

Great Answer: "To be honest, I enjoy both. No person works entirely as an individual, an island, unless he or she owns a business and is the sole employee. In pharmaceutical sales, I'm responsible for my own success or failure; yet as a member of a team, I can also gain support from others and gain comfort from the fact that we are all working toward the common goal of extending and enhancing human lives through the products we sell. Yes, I have a great deal of competitive spirit, and it has spurred my success. But I also know that in a team environment, we can share ideas, knowledge, and techniques with each other and everyone (individually) benefits. If one team member has a fantastic relationship with a physician that others find difficult to access, why not draw upon that rep's knowledge and techniques for the benefit of all? In addition, teamwork inspires each member to grow in ability and knowledge. What happens, then, when all members are inspired to reach their full potential? It raises the bar and adds to the competitive spirit that must be present for each individual to succeed. In a climate that is both supportive and competitive, each individual will strive to reach his or her maximum potential."

Your Response:_____

_____

_____

_____

_____

**Have you ever worked in
a team-selling environment?**

What They're Really Trying to Determine: Have you had to work in an environment where everyone must contribute in order for the team to succeed? If you performed successfully in this type of an environment, the manager will be confident you will be successful as a pharma rep.

What Not to Do: Stating that you've never worked in this type of environment is not a choice. It simply will not gain you the job; nor is it entirely true.

Your Plan: Show how you've worked in a team-selling environment, even if this experience was not associated with a specific job. You must examine every job you've worked, sports you've played or coached, schools you've attended, volunteer experience or family responsibilities you've had, and so on. At one point in your life, you must have had to work for the good of a team ... so start thinking! And, you don't have to limit yourself to those experiences in which you sold a product. Rather, you may have team-sold an idea or a solution to a problem.

Great Answer: "As a member of my college volleyball team, I worked as part of a team to accomplish a larger goal. In particular, we were always looking for ways to earn money for our volleyball program. As team captain, I created and organized a number of fundraisers, including silent auctions, sales of T-shirts and candy bars, and summer volleyball training camps for children. Although the ultimate reward was creating funding for the volleyball department, we were a competitive bunch. So we began competing against each other to see who could raise the largest sum of money. Because we had all played sports together, we knew it would take great individual efforts to accomplish team success. Although many of these fundraisers cut into our limited recreational time, we placed the good of the team above our own interests. Due to our incredible teamwork and determination, our fundraisers were a huge success. In one year, we raised more money for the volleyball department than had previously been raised in the previous five. Little did we realize that we were learning important selling and teamwork skills, because it was so much fun!"

*Your Response:*_____

_____

_____

_____

_____

PFIZER! PFIZER! PFIZER!

A Pfizer manager asked an interviewee: *"Do you work better as an individual or as a team?"*

The interviewee answered with: *"I work well as an individual or as a part of a team."*

The manager replied with: *"Choose one."*

My customer answered with: *"As an individual."*

The manager replied with: *"We work in teams here."*

What is synergy, and how can it be applied to pharmaceutical sales?

What They're Really Trying to Determine: Your general beliefs and knowledge of how teamwork can accomplish goals. They're also testing your industry and pharma sales knowledge regarding the synergy of drugs.

Your Plan: Demonstrate your knowledge of the effects of drug synergy as well as the effectiveness of synergy within a sales organization and between two different sales organizations with shared goals and strategies.

Great Answer: "With reference to drug synergy, "synergy" means the combined action of two or more drugs working together more effectively than either drug working alone. With reference to synergy within pharmaceutical sales organizations, synergy is created when everyone works together as a sales team rather than everyone working entirely independently and without regard for other team members. This type of synergy is necessary for organizational survival and success. Synergy may also refer to the effects of co-promotion, in which two different companies enter into an agreement to promote the same product. By coordinating the efforts of two sales forces with a common goal and strategy, synergy is created and profits are greatly increased."

Your Response: _____

_____

_____

_____

_____

Imagine you're on a team with FIVE other sales professionals. For the two months, you've done all the planning (creating team goals for the new quarter, completing team assignments from the district manager, and so on) and accomplished all other team tasks entirely on your own. You feel your teammates are relying on you too much and that they're not doing their fair share. What would you do?

What They're Really Trying to Determine: How well do you work in teams? Can you handle the "people problems" that arise in a team environment?

What Not to Do: Don't respond that you would take the problem immediately to your manager; that approach shows a lack of problem-solving skills.

Your Plan: Have a detailed plan of action, and show your willingness to creatively work through "people issues".

Great Answer: "First, I'd 'suck it up' for a while. It might be that personal issues are affecting my teammates' performance, and I'm assuming that we've developed a relationship that involves picking up the slack for each other when that is needed. That's what an effective and cohesive team does. If the situation continues long enough to cause damage to our team, our district, and/or our customers, however, then I would bring my concern to the attention of my teammates. Maybe they're having a tough time with family issues that prevent them from doing their job in its entirety, or maybe they have additional job responsibilities that I was unaware of. Perhaps all I would need to do is alert them to the issue and they would rectify it. In the end, if the issue isn't rectified, I would ask the advice of my manager as to how to proceed. I might also need to remind myself that just because I set such high expectations for myself doesn't mean that others do, as well. Many times I may have to be the leader and do much more of the work than the others simply because I have the desire and means to do so."

Your Response: _____

_____

_____

_____

_____

> *Talking and eloquence are not the same: To speak, and to speak well, are two things. A fool may talk, but a wise man speaks.*
>
> —BEN JONSON

Interview Questions and GREAT Answers that Show Your Coachability and Loyalty

Managers want to know that you are willing to learn, to follow, and to be led.

By asking these questions, they are seeking answers that will prove whether you are a good fit with their management style.

6. Does your current manager provide help and leadership to you in your position?

What They're Really Trying to Determine: What is your relationship with management? Do you display negativity toward authority or leadership? Are you coachable and willing to learn from others?

What Not to Do: Do not criticize your current manager or any previous managers.

Your Plan: Answer this question in a positive manner. Think of all the positives you can with regard to management traits and styles.

Great Answer: "I appreciate my manager's constructive criticism because I know it has helped me further hone my sales techniques. When a knowledgeable professional takes the time to offer constructive criticism, I make it a priority to sit down and listen … and then swiftly to put that advice into action. I also appreciate my manager's (utilize any of the following and provide examples)

    a. direction and support, with a fair amount of freedom to accomplish goals.

    b. motivational and positive attitude.

    c. creation of a supportive work environment that encourages creativity.

    d. creation of a work environment that rewards exceptional results.

    e. fair treatment of subordinates.

    f. patience and ability to teach and coach others to success.

    g. team-building skills that inspire us to work for the good of the team.

    h. ability to hire talented professionals who work as a cohesive team.

    i. keen ability to recognize each individual's strengths."

Your Response: _____

_____

_____

_____

_____

Who was the best boss you've ever had, and why?

What They're Trying to Determine: Are you teachable? What sort of management style do you like and work best under?

What Not to Do: Stating "I haven't really had any good bosses …" is not a good idea. Nor is it good to list the negatives of a former boss without specifically being asked to. Highlight only the positives.

Your Plan: Highlight the positive traits of a previous manager that relate well to what is expected in pharma sales jobs.

Great Answer: "My first boss had a way of guiding and mentoring her reps, without making us feel like we were being 'managed'. This inspired us to be more creative and better problem solvers because we felt she had given us everything we needed—the tools to be successful on our own. In addition, she was there to listen and advise whenever called upon. She also insisted on a healthy work/life balance. I believe we experienced great results partly due to those aspects of her management style."

Your Response: _____

_____

_____

_____

_____

Can you handle criticism? How do you react to it?

What They're Really Trying to Determine: Can you handle constructive criticism? Are you coachable, or do you reject authority?

What Not to Do: Do not show that you are a loose cannon or that you are so sensitive that any type of criticism deeply wounds you. Displaying a negative reaction to this question will also hurt you.

Your Plan: In your answer, you must show that you are eager to learn from managers, acknowledging that their experience and knowledge is far greater than yours. You must demonstrate that your goal is to develop into a better sales professional and that you appreciate constructive criticism because it helps you reach that goal more swiftly.

Great Answer: "I appreciate it when those who are more knowledgeable and experienced than myself offer constructive criticism. Although it may not always be easy to hear *(showing your human side is good)*, it is always appreciated because it helps me become a more competent professional. Once I'm provided with constructive feedback about a mistake, I make a conscious attempt to not make that error ever again. Learning is an important part of my professional development, and I'm grateful when professionals take time out of their busy days to provide constructive assessment of my job performance. In addition, learning new methods and acquiring new knowledge is exciting to me and keeps me motivated to go to work every day. I am open to input and dedicated to improvement; therefore, I am able to benefit from constructive criticism."

Your Response: _____

_____

_____

_____

_____

9. **What would you change about your current manager's style of management?**

What They're Really Trying to Determine: Your perception of management in general. Are you a team player? Are you a positive and loyal employee?

What Not to Do: Do not give negative responses. The manager will think that if you were hired and someday were looking for a position outside the company, you would speak negatively of him or her. A negative attitude also speaks volumes about your lack of loyalty.

Your Plan: Concentrate on your manager's strengths and positive attributes. Minimize weaknesses, even if there are many. Select only a fairly minor weakness to discuss. Also, utilize the sandwich technique: begin with a positive, insert the negative into the middle of the response, and end with a positive. This works for any negatively oriented interview question. In addition, utilizing the pronoun "we" helps deflect a little of the negativity, as if you're taking some responsibility for the problem. This shows that you are loyal and a great team player.

Great Answer: "My current boss is an exceptional leader who has gained the respect of his team and motivates us to perform to our best potential. The only 'weakness' I have witnessed is his inability to know when to stop coaching (in other words, when to give up) and just allow someone to fail because of their own incompetence. On one occasion, we lost focus of the big picture, and it began to drain many of our resources. On the other hand, I think it's a commendable quality to be willing to give of oneself to help someone grow professionally and personally. His 'never say die' attitude has enabled each of us to surpass goals that we may never have reached on our own."

Your Response: _____

_____

_____

_____

_____

10. Does your current manager motivate you to perform your job to the maximum of your potential? How are you motivated?

What They're Trying to Determine: How are you empowered to perform to the best of your capabilities? This helps the manager know if you'll succeed under his or her management style.

What Not to Do: Don't list the negative qualities of your manager; concentrate only on the positive. If, for example, your manager is not a technical person, you may want to comment on his exceptional people skills. Also, don't list any motivating qualities that you're confident the hiring manager does *not* have. This will only count against you and make the manager feel inferior.

Your Plan: Make a list of all qualities you like (and are motivated by) in a manager. Now, from the list, pick the two or three qualities that you've realized (through research with other employees or during the course of the interview) this manager has. Don't just list qualities, however. You should also explain why those qualities motivate you and give an example of a success that can be attributed to your manager's specific attribute.

Great Answer: (Let's assume you made your list of qualities that motivate you. During the conversation with the hiring manager, you notice that this manager has given several examples of how he or she leads by example, so you reply as follows.) "My current manager is a great leader. Because he leads by example and has such a positive attitude, we all respect him and are inspired to succeed. As a result of this, I've felt empowered to take risks—within the boundaries of company guidelines—and push myself out of my comfort zone in order to reach and surpass the aggressive goals he has set for me. For example, I created and developed a new marketing plan based on a previous companywide marketing plan … but with a few new twists. I aggressively targeted realtors—who had previously been left out of the marketing equation—and experienced little success, at first. After contacting 35 to 40 realtors, I finally hit 'pay dirt'. I negotiated a lucrative deal with one of the oldest and best known realtors in our town. Then, I utilized his endorsement and influence to win over many of the realtors I had originally prospected. *(Just like pharma reps do when they win over an "opinion leader physician".)* This success resulted in allowing me to hit my goals, only five months into the year. Had I not had a manager to back me up, I probably wouldn't have had the resolve to go after a new market. It was a risky move that could have eaten up a lot of my time, without good results. However, my manager's 'nothing ventured, nothing gained' philosophy really resonated with me and I believe ensures my success today." *(Meaning that you'll not work like that only at your old job, but you'll succeed no matter where you work or whom you work with!)*

Your Response: _____

_____

_____

_____

_____

> *The worst mistake a boss can make is not to say "well done".*
>
> —JOHN ASHCROFT

11. Describe your relationship with your last three supervisors.

What They're Trying to Determine: Similar to the earlier questions: How do you deal with authority? Are you coachable?

What Not to Do: Do not describe three "perfect" managers and the "perfect" relationship you had with each of them. This would just not be a realistic picture, and the manager would doubt your honesty.

Your Plan: Describe two of the three managers as "good," and describe their qualities and the positive relationships you had with them. Describe the third as someone with whom you had some differences of opinion but from whom you still learned a great deal. Provide examples of what you've learned.

Great Answer: "Two of my last three managers were exceptional. They both understood how to lead by example and empower their people. They also felt confident enough to ask questions and learn from their people. We had a great partnership and learned volumes from each other. My managers viewed me as a competent partner, not a subordinate that had to be monitored every second of the day. That really inspired me to gain an 'entrepreneurial mindset' and enabled me to be in charge of my own sales territory for which I, alone, determined the success or failure *(just like a pharmaceutical sales rep must do)*. I began to take real ownership of my responsibilities, and I immediately noticed greater results. The third manager was a great salesperson, but he seemed to have difficulties establishing and growing relationships with his people. Although we frequently held differences of opinion, we both respected each other. In fact, once his decision was made on a controversial issue, I always backed it, and he always valued that."

Your Response: _____

_____

_____

_____

_____

12. Tell me about a time when your honesty and/or integrity caused a problem for you and what you did to resolve it.

What They're Trying to Determine: Are you an ethical person who makes good judgments based upon the situation? Do you follow through on your promises?

What Not to Do: Don't focus on a large problem. And don't intimate that you're difficult to work with or that the problem caused a rift in a relationship with a coworker, manager, or customer.

Your Plan: Focus on a small, relatively insignificant problem that had a positive outcome.

Great Answer: "As a former baseball coach, I occasionally had to take disciplinary action when players chose to make poor decisions regarding their free time. Sometimes my disciplinary action was not well received by some of the more fanatical parents who didn't appreciate their son sitting out a game. Regardless of the parental outcry, I had to treat inappropriate behavior in a consistent and fair manner. Although some parents initially were agitated and made it a point to let me know it, I always was able to minimize the problems by responding to them in a direct and open manner, no matter how busy I was. As a result, the misbehavior decreased among my players as they witnessed the consistency of rules and discipline. In addition, the parents came to expect and respect my integrity … in that I always did what I said I would do and never wavered when faced with outside pressure."

Your Response: _____

_____

_____

_____

_____

Interview Questions with GREAT Answers that Showcase and Assess Your Goal-Driven Attitude, Behavior, and Leadership Qualities

13. What are your career goals?

What They're Trying to Determine: Are you goal oriented? Do your career goals match what the company has to offer?

What Not to Do: Do not mention goals that you know the organization cannot help you attain.

Your Plan: Make sure to sound clear and definite when discussing your career goals, but also base your answer on what you know about the organization. Mention only those goals that you feel the organization can help you achieve. Consider the experience you hope to gain and the expertise you hope to develop. Leave the impression that your desire to grow as a professional is realistic, just as your promotion and salary expectations are.

Great Answer: "I feel that I have an excellent background with exceptional accomplishments, notable communication skills, and a large repertoire of sales skills *(express your current skills)*. Working in pharmaceutical sales will allow me to further hone those skills *(express your desire to learn more)*. Pharmaceutical sales is considered the ultimate sales job. I'm really looking for a good challenge and a position in which I can grow my sales skills and be totally responsible for my own success—putting some cash in my pocket while also providing tremendous profitability for the company. Knowing that I'm an essential part of a pharmaceutical company's success is very motivating in that I'll play a role in extending and enhancing people's lives. That's powerful. In looking at my interview portfolio, you'll note that I have a career goals summary. *(Show the applicable page in your brag book, and state your career goals, including timelines.)*"

Your Response: _____

_____

_____

_____

_____

How do you handle rejection?

What They're Trying to Determine: Pharmaceutical reps are faced with rejection on a daily basis. The interviewer wants to be assured that you can persevere in these situations.

What Not to Do: Don't say that you don't handle rejection well.

Your Plan: Show that you have handled rejection in the past and explain what you may have learned from the experience.

Great Answer: "I realize that rejection is a part of sales, and I do not take rejection personally. In my current position, I deal with rejection frequently. I analyze every situation and try to grow from it. I try to figure out why they rejected my offer and come up with a new plan for my next visit. In my opinion, rejection is an opportunity to sell. If every call was easy, with every person on every call being willing to give me 100 percent of their business, that would take the fun and challenge out of selling. I thrive on overcoming rejection and ultimately making the sale."

Your Response: _____

_____

_____

_____

_____

15. What do you think determines a person's progress with a good company?

What They're Trying to Determine: Your work values and your commitment to them.

What Not to Do: Don't focus on other people; rather, state what you can do, personally, to ensure success.

Your Plan: Respond positively with common work values. Make sure you can provide examples of where and how you've exhibited those values within the workplace.

Great Answer: "I think determination and hard work, integrity, intelligence, excellent communication skills, and the ability to sell ideas and get results are what determine your progress. In my past sales job, I was promoted twice to positions of more responsibility due to my dedication to the job and always going the extra mile. In addition to the qualities an employee should exhibit, I believe that a company should have competitive products, effective management, a commitment to its customers, and a reward program to recognize employees' exceptional performance."

Your Response: _____

_____

_____

_____

_____

NEVER LIE ON YOUR RÉSUMÉ

Years ago, you may have been able to "fudge" some of the information on your résumé and get away with it. Today, don't even think about trying it. All companies verify the details on applicants' résumés.

16. What personal, non-job-related goals have you set for yourself?

What They're Trying to Determine: Are you a thoughtful person? Have you taken the time to consider your life goals—both job-related and non-work-related goals? Are you committed to personal growth?

What Not to Do: Don't give your interviewer the idea that you live for your work. All managers realize the value of a well-rounded employee who values his or her personal time. If you show that you're a workaholic, they'll fear you'll be at risk for burnout.

Your Plan: Goals related to your family are always acceptable, and sometimes preferred, because they demonstrate stability. In addition, anything related to personal growth, such as taking night classes, setting physical fitness goals, learning a foreign language, and so on, is a good answer.

Great Answer: "Some of my goals relate to my personal development. For example, I want to get my MBA within the next couple of years. I will take Saturday classes to accomplish that because gaining an advanced degree is something I've always wanted to do. Although this is a personal goal, I know it will help me immensely in my professional life, as well.

Some of my other personal goals are related to my family. I want to add to my child's academic development and spend quality time with him. I'm learning Spanish with my four-year-old son—and he's soaking it up much faster than I am! I'm hoping I can learn from *him* (*humor is good*). Also, with the coming New Year, I've renewed my physical fitness goals. I'm currently training to run in the next Dam to Dam race. My ultimate fitness goal is to compete in a marathon; to me, it would symbolize real accomplishment in terms of mental attitude and physical performance."

Your Response: _____

_____

_____

_____

_____

17. What have you done to increase your personal development?

What They're Really Trying to Determine: Similarly to the last question, they're trying to determine if you are committed to growth on both a personal and a professional level.

What Not to Do: As in the preceding question, don't indicate that you're all work and no play. This makes for an unhappy employee who performs average work.

Your Plan: Demonstrate your willingness to stretch yourself personally and how this indirectly relates to your professional development. Consider classes, professional clubs, special training or research, books you've read, and so on.

Great Answer: "I'm an avid reader, especially of books regarding sales prospecting, question-based selling, and the art of closing. Some of my favorite books are: *Swim With the Sharks Without Being Eaten Alive* by Harvey Mackay, and *Secrets of Question-Based Selling,* by Thomas Freese. *(Read them. They are invaluable for pharma sales.)* As a former business owner, I began reading these books and quickly realized how much I enjoy them. As a result of this reading, I've developed into a more positive person with a 'can-do' attitude about every goal I set for myself. It has helped me succeed both personally and professionally. I'm also a big fan of public speaking, so I've been working on that skill as well. I've been a member of our area Toastmasters Club for a little over two years. It has helped me develop into a better communicator as well as a more relaxed and confident salesperson. Little did I know that it would be a great team-building experience, as well! As an elder member of the club, I now teach my public speaking skills to new members, which I thoroughly enjoy."

Your Response: _____

_____

_____

_____

_____

18. What is the most important lesson you've learned in the last TEN years?

What They're Really Trying to Determine: Are you a person who is retrospective, who looks behind—in addition to looking forward—to learn from past mistakes and successes?

What Not to Do: Don't give any routine, cheesy answers about kindness, love, caring, understanding, empathy, and so on. Although seemingly unimportant, the answer to this question can tell a manager volumes about how you choose to live your life.

Your Plan: Choose a lesson that relates to both your personal and your professional life. This increases the value of the lesson learned.

Great Answer: "Because of my passion for reading books about sales techniques, I've learned a valuable lesson: Sales skills help you succeed in every area of life. My relationships with family, managers and coworkers, friends, and clients have literally been transformed. Why? Because the number-one rule in sales is to be a good listener and uncover the other person's needs and wants. Sounds like a great relationship builder, right? I find it especially revealing that Stephen Chandler's book, *50 Ways to Create Great Relationships,* is most popular among the demographic of women who love Dr. Phil and Oprah. Little do they realize that it was first and foremost meant to be a how-to book for salespeople. But once you read it, it reveals the parallel between everyday relationships and the salesman/prospect/client relationship. I feel that by being a student of sales methodology, I've become a more fulfilled person in all aspects of my life—personal and professional."

Your Response: _____

_____

_____

_____

_____

TWO WAYS TO MAKE A FRIEND
OF YOUR INTERVIEWER

1. Be sure to tell the person you interviewed with that you would enjoy working with him or her. The manager will definitely be looking to hire someone with whom they can get along well.

2. Most people don't send a handwritten note after an interview, and that's a mistake. You may even want to prewrite a note. If the interview is at a hotel, you can leave the note at the front desk for your interviewer.

What are two qualities that help you succeed and two qualities you must work on to achieve your career goals?

What They're Really Trying to Determine: How well do you know yourself? Are you aware of your positives as well as the personal road-blocks you must conquer in order to succeed?

What Not to Do: This question is *not* asking you to reveal negatives but simply to discuss those skills you may need to improve upon to reach your goals.

Your Plan: Back up the four qualities/skills with rich examples to support your assertions. Lead with the qualities you need to improve upon, and finish with the "good stuff."

Great Answer: "The two qualities I could improve upon really depend on the goals I want to achieve. We all have things we must improve upon at any given time. If we didn't, how would we ever learn and grow? When I opened my franchise, I probably would have succeeded more quickly if I had set up a formal marketing system to advertise my business. I would say that in my haste to start working and make money, I didn't create a long-term marketing strategy and later had to make major adjustments to compensate for it. The other quality I must improve upon is taking the time to evaluate what I've done, where I'm going, and what I can learn from the past. I think that when you slow down and do this, you are able to accomplish goals more effectively and efficiently. Because of my high energy and enthusiasm for my work, I tend not to take as much time as I should to plan long-term strategies and to reflect/learn from the past. Regarding my two positive qualities, my communication skills and goal-driven determination have helped me succeed in all of my career endeavors. Exceptional communication skills enabled me to run a successful business that responded quickly to customer needs and wants and focused on rapport-building within the community as well as with my clients. When I noted that sales were beginning to stagnate, I set new goals for myself and was determined to double my sales volume from the previous year. This is when I came up with my realtor referral program, which quickly sparked sales and continued to do so for the entire time I owned the business."

Your Response: _____

_____

_____

_____

_____

20.

How long will it take before you make a positive contribution to our organization?

What They're Really Trying to Determine: What do you know about our company and our industry? Do you know enough to set realistic goals for yourself?

What Not to Do: Don't be unrealistic about the kind of contribution you can make and the length of time it will take you to accomplish it. This will count more against you than anything else; it will also show your ignorance of the industry.

Your Plan: Reveal a positive, confident attitude, and show your knowledge of the duties of a pharmaceutical rep.

Great Answer: "I think my partner, my team, and you *(the manager)* will notice my contribution right away. I've always been told that my excitement is contagious. My team-building skills, positive and determined attitude, and unparalleled commitment to succeed are positive contributions I'll make immediately upon joining your team. Of course, I'll commit a lot of time and effort to training, learning the territory, and becoming familiar with each medical facility's guidelines. I believe it's realistic to expect that within six months the results of my exceptional communication skills and 'never say die' attitude will show forth in my increased access to physicians and increased volume of new scripts."

Your Response: _____

_____

_____

_____

_____

21. What is your greatest strength?

What They're Really Trying to Determine: What's your number-one skill, asset, or strength? Can you analyze yourself? Is your number-one skill, asset, or strength transferable to pharmaceutical sales?

What Not to Do: Don't waiver. Be clear and concise with your answer. Don't use one-word answers, and remember to provide proof through examples.

Your Plan: Going into the interview, you should have in mind several strengths that directly relate to pharmaceutical sales. Begin with a brief statement of one of those skills or abilities, and then provide a clear example. Choosing a broad category, such as communication skills, allows you to discuss several other important attributes that fall under that category. In essence, you'll be able to discuss many of your strengths, instead of just one. It's a nifty little trick that can be used with great success!

Great Answer: "I believe that my communication skills are my greatest strength. When people think of communication skills, they are often unaware of all that goes into being a good communicator. For example, a good communicator can engage a listener. A good communicator is also an exceptional listener. Good communication involves presentation and negotiation skills as well as the ability to anticipate needs, empathize, and influence. Because of my strong communication skills, I've led my sales team for two years in a row and have blown out many of my yearly sales goals within the first eight months. How have I accomplished this? (1) By being an exceptional listener—determining my client's wants and needs. (2) By becoming a partner to my client—being a 'knowledge source' and presenting unique ideas about how to implement my products and benefit his/her clients. (3) By utilizing a repertoire of sales techniques—negotiation, empathy, influence, and engagement. What's the number-one reason for this success? Very simply, it's my strong communication skills."

Your Response: _____

_____

_____

_____

_____

22. What are your THREE most important career achievements?

What They're Really Trying to Determine: Do the career successes you choose to highlight naturally transfer to pharmaceutical sales jobs? Do the successes you choose to highlight show that your interests and values are a good match for pharmaceutical sales jobs?

What Not to Do: Do not choose successes that do not demonstrate skills required in pharmaceutical sales jobs. Don't ramble; take about 45 to 60 seconds to explain each accomplishment.

Your Plan: Utilize the STAR format—(situation•task•action•result)—to explain your successes. Then choose the most important of your achievements and explain how the skills involved mirrored the skills needed for pharmaceutical sales.

Great Answer: *(First, provide a quick synopsis of the first two accomplishments. Then end with something like the following.)* "As an HR generalist in a company that was facing extreme budget constraints, I was asked to analyze our HR vendor contracts and implement cost-saving measures. I redesigned the employee time-card system, researched the best vendor to develop my system, and negotiated price concessions. I then implemented the system through employee training sessions—and accomplished all of this within my six-month deadline. As a result, I saved the company over $18,000 per year in vendor payouts for human resource functions. This accomplishment required many of the same skills I'd utilize as a pharmaceutical sales rep, such as:

1. The ability to come up with **creative solutions** to a budgetary problem.
2. Exceptional **presentation skills** in communicating our needs and wants to vendors, training employees, and presenting my plan to company executives for approval.
3. **Negotiation skills** in gaining price concessions from outside HR vendors.
4. **Organization skills** played a key role in this accomplishment. Analyzing our current systems; keeping track of vendor proposals; creating and following an aggressive, detailed timeline; establishing a training system—all required exceptional organization skills."

Your Response: _____

_____

_____

_____

_____

Only undertake what you can do in an excellent fashion. There are no prizes for average performance.

—BRIAN TRACY

24. Why have you decided to pursue a career in pharmaceutical sales?

What They're Trying to Determine: Have you thought this through? Do your interests relate to aspects of pharmaceutical sales work? Are your skills and experience related to pharmaceutical sales work?

What Not to Do: PUHHHLEASE don't focus on benefits, salary, bonuses, trips, and so forth.

Your Plan: Merge your interests, skills, and qualities with various aspects of pharmaceutical sales jobs.

Great Answer: Most important, mention that you love to sell and that you've been very successful in sales. *(Even if you do not have typical sales experience, you can provide examples of times when you've utilized sales skills to negotiate, persuade, influence, and so on.)* Provide specific, concrete examples of sales success.

You love the fact that the pharmaceutical sales industry offers both challenge and reward. The technical aspect of the science behind the products appeals to you. *(Cite examples of how well you've performed in technical courses or environments.)* Also, you like the fact that you're responsible and rewarded for your own success, but that there's also a team environment in which you work to sell your product. *(Give examples of situations in which you thrived on your own, and then provide examples of being a team player and achieving a goal.)* To answer this question effectively, you must know exactly what a pharmaceutical sales rep does on a daily basis.

Summary of a Typical Day
(For additional information and more detail, visit Anne's website at www.pharmaceutical-rep.com.)

- You start the night before by planning out your day and setting your call objectives for each prescriber you plan to detail.
- You call on 4 to 6 prescribers in the morning to help ensure that you complete your 8 to 10 calls by the end of the day. You also enter post-call notes after each visit.
- Next, you attend a lunch and learn program at one of the offices on your target list.
- In the afternoon, you complete seeing your scheduled offices based on the routing schedule developed by your team.
- Finally, you end your busy day by attending a dinner program that you or your team planned several months in advance. You will be able to get feedback on the information the speaker presented to attending prescribers the next time you call on them.

Next, show your knowledge of the industry. *(It's a growing industry due to the fact that baby boomers are reaching retirement. This will result in an increasing need for pharmaceuticals to enrich and extend lives.)* Provide some industry statistics to back up your statements. Most hiring managers love statistics! Find information at www.phrma.org (PhRMA—for Everything Pertaining to the Pharmaceutical Industry!).

Finally, show your knowledge of the pharmaceutical company *(you'd better have done some research!)* and state that you will be very selective about the company you choose to work with. Obviously there needs to be a good fit between the company and candidate in order for both to be successful. Provide specific reasons that the company is a good fit for you.

Your Response: _____

_____

_____

_____

_____

25. Which do you value more, monetary reward for achievements or the feeling of knowing you're the best?

What They're Trying to Determine: How are you motivated, extrinsically (by money, awards, and so on) or intrinsically (by wanting to be the best regardless of the external rewards)?

What Not to Do: Don't focus on one form of motivation over the other. Combine the two for the best answer.

Your Plan: Reflect on the fact that you're motivated to be the best but that you also appreciate money and awards as recognition for your accomplishments.

Great Answer: "I've always had very high standards and have pushed myself to be the very best, regardless of the rewards. I'm motivated intrinsically to be the best, and I greatly enjoy the challenge as well as the feeling of accomplishment that goes along with it. However, I'm human, and like most other people, I'm also motivated by the promise of external rewards such as money, awards, acknowledgement, trips, and opportunities to advance in my career. Therefore, I would say that I value both and that both spur me to accomplish my goals. This is why I believe that a pharmaceutical sales career is a good match for me—it offers a generous supply of challenge, opportunity, and reward!"

Your Response: _____

_____

_____

_____

_____

26. How do you know you'll succeed in pharmaceutical sales?

What They're Trying to Determine: Are you confident you'll succeed? If so, make us confident through this answer. Prove to us that you have the knowledge, skills, and experience to be successful in this career.

What Not to Do: Don't simply say "yes" without backing that up with examples as proof. This will not inspire confidence.

Your Plan/Great Answer: List the key skills required to be successful in pharmaceutical sales—good communication skills, tenacity and determination, sales/teaching background, ability to understand and present technical information, being coachable in terms of learning the selling process and further developing your skills, being a team player, competitive drive, entrepreneurial spirit, being a self-starter, and so on. Then provide a simple example of how you possess each of these skills. Also, provide examples of situations in which you've had to work on your own (as is the case in pharma sales jobs), and describe how that's been a successful and/or profitable experience.

Your Response: _____

_____

_____

_____

_____

27. What motivates you to go to work every day?

What They're Trying to Determine: Can you handle working in a team environment while at the same time being responsible for yourself? Pharmaceutical sales managers do not have time to "baby-sit" their reps.

What Not to Do: Don't say that you've never had a job in which you've had to work on your own or indicate that you've worked only with micromanagers.

Your Plan/Great Answer: Discuss that your intrinsic motivation to be the best at whatever you do is what motivates you to go to work every day. Indicate that you don't need a manager looking over your shoulder and that your competitive spirit drives you to go above and beyond in every task or job you take on. Emphasize that as a pharma rep, you'll have your own territory and will be responsible for your own success or failure—and that this is very motivating to you. Provide an example of how you've gone above and beyond normal duties and expectations in your previous or current job.

Your Response: _____

_____

_____

_____

_____

Vice presidents and personnel directors of the 100 largest corporations were asked to describe their most unusual experience interviewing prospective employees. Here are some of their answers.

- A job applicant challenged the interviewer to an arm wrestle.
- The interviewee wore a Walkman, explaining that she could listen to the interviewer and the music at the same time.
- The candidate fell and broke his arm during the interview.
- The candidate announced that she hadn't had lunch and proceeded to eat a hamburger and French fries in the interviewer's office.
- The candidate explained that her long-term goal was to replace the interviewer.
- The candidate said he never finished high school because he was kidnapped and kept in a closet in Mexico.
- A balding candidate excused himself and returned to the office a few minutes later wearing a hairpiece.
- The applicant said that if he was hired he would demonstrate his loyalty by having the corporate logo tattooed on his forearm.
- The applicant interrupted the interview to phone her therapist for advice on how to answer specific interview questions.
- The candidate brought a large dog to the interview.

- The applicant refused to sit down, insisting on being interviewed standing up.
- The candidate dozed off during the interview.

28. How long do you expect to work as a primary care rep before being promoted?

What They're Trying to Determine: Do you have realistic expectations? Are you knowledgeable enough about this industry to provide a reasonable answer?

What Not to Do: Don't be overconfident and say that you should be able to be promoted within a year because you're some sort of "sales dynamo". This is not a realistic expectation, and the interviewing manager will think you lack maturity.

Your Plan/Great Answer: Simply state that you have mapped out a career path for yourself, and from what you've determined (through research with other reps and books), you feel it is realistic to be promoted to a specialty position within two to three and a half years, contingent upon exceptional success.

Your Response: _____

_____

_____

_____

_____

PHARMACEUTICAL SALES CAREER PATHS

Although pharma sales is one of the most sought after and rewarding careers in the United States, many reps stumble into it, having begun with little or no idea of what a pharma career is all about. Nevertheless, many successful executives began as territory reps. The following are some career path options that pharma sales reps take.

Sales Opportunities

At most pharma companies, the sales team has a hierarchical structure that consists of territory representatives, specialty and hospital representatives, district managers or regional sales directors, a regional manager or area business manager, national account managers, and regional account managers.

Sales Training and Development Opportunities

Sales training and development offers a wide variety of career options for motivated representatives who are ready for a new challenge. Sales training candidates tend to be self-motivated, successful representatives who have enjoyed their work in the field and would like to share their ideas and experience with the sales force.

Marketing Opportunities

Marketing is all about teamwork—from working with strategic therapeutic area teams and licensing/business development to develop commercially viable products to collaborating with sales, sales training, sales administration, medical, law, and customer service to ensure that new products are successfully brought to market.

Managed Care Opportunities

The responsibilities of an account executive are multidimensional and exciting. Managed care account executives apply the skills they developed as sales representatives, such as multitasking and networking, to increase and maintain formulary coverage in managed care and alternative health care markets. They make calls on business managers and other decision makers in managed care organizations and long-term care facilities, state offices impacting Medicaid, and state agencies and associations.

29. How stressed or pressured do you feel about sales goals?

What They're Trying to Determine: Can you handle the pressures inherent in this job? Sales reps are expected to reach 100 percent of their target, and if the particular product is especially strong, numbers should extend past 100 percent. Pharma sales is a high–profile career, and if you're not making your numbers, there are plenty of other candidates ready and willing to take your place.

What Not to Do: This is not the time or place to discuss how ineffectively you handle stress. Nor do you want to mention any mental, physical, or emotional problems triggered by stress. Your job is to appear confident and capable.

Your Plan/Great Answer: "I do feel pressured by sales goals ... but it's a good kind of pressure—the kind that brings out my tenaciousness and challenges me to exceed expectations. The more pressured I feel, the more organized I become. Knowing that a deadline or goal is near, I'm better able to prioritize, act quickly on my feet, and engage more than ever my determination to reach and surpass my goals. To be honest, stress and pressure bring out my competitive spirit in full force. For example ... *(provide an example, in STAR format, of a situation in which you felt pressured or stressed and how you rose to the occasion).*"

Your Response: _____

_____

_____

_____

_____

30. Are you willing to work past 5:00 p.m. or in the evenings? Are you willing to relocate?

What They're Trying to Determine: How committed are you to this career and this company?

What Not to Do: An inflexible response will not demonstrate commitment to your career. At this point, the manager is basically asking if you're interested enough in the company to work overtime or make a move. Rarely are people asked to relocate upon being hired by a company.

Great Answer (working late): "I am committed to working every day until the job is done. I'm aware that pharma reps often have to work early in the morning or on Saturdays at hospital displays or trade shows. I'm also aware that team meetings, training, or speaker programs often require working during the evening. I am willing to work as hard and as long as is necessary to achieve and exceed my sales goals." *(Provide an example of your determination and hard work in a previous position.)*

Great Answer (willingness to relocate): Obviously, if you're willing to relocate, then say so; but if you're not, don't hurt yourself by saying you're unwilling to do so. Ninety-nine percent of new hires are never asked to relocate—it really is extremely rare. Instead, try this: "I'm very excited about working for your company because *(give two facts you've found through research)*. I definitely have an open mind about relocating, if the opportunity is right. Please note, however, that in this particular area I have a large network of physicians with whom I already have established great relationships. Of course, I'll keep an open mind about great opportunities within this company, even if it means relocating. That's how strongly I feel about working for your company."

Your Response: _____

_____

_____

_____

_____

31. If you are hired, where do you see yourself in 6 months? and in years 5 and 10?

What They're Trying to Determine: As in earlier questions, the manager is trying to determine how knowledgeable you are about this career and how realistic you are about your career goals.

What Not to Do: Don't be general or evasive; be specific in terms of what you're going to do and where you want your career to go. This will show your in-depth industry knowledge and prove that you are serious about your career choice.

Your Plan/Great Answer: A good way to begin to answer this question would be to show the manager your 90-day plan *(see below for a good example)*. Next, explain what you will accomplish in the first 6 months and what your career goals are for years 5 and 10. Qualify your assertions of what you will be doing in years 5 and 10 by affirming your awareness that attainment of these positions will be based upon your determination to succeed and a history of success with exceptional national rankings.

Your Response: _____

_____

_____

_____

_____

90-Day Plan of Action

GOAL 1:
Successfully complete training. EXCEED expectations.

GOAL 2:
Become familiar with established territory, and meet
with partners and managers.

GOAL 3:
Research the status of my territory.

GOAL 4:
Understand the local status of my products in hospitals
and doctors' offices.

GOAL 5:
Understand and become familiar with the status of the formulary.

GOAL 6:
Know who my major customers are: Who are the 20 percent
who will give me 80 percent of my business?

GOAL 7:
Research my competition and my competing products.

GOAL 8:
Work with my counterparts. Join them in meetings and calls.

GOAL 9:
Develop a strategic plan of action, and set goals for my daily sales calls.

GOAL 10:
Act on my training and become a blockbuster sales representative!

32. Tell me about a time when you were selected to be a leader. What happened?

What They're Trying to Determine: Are you comfortable taking a leadership role? Pharma sales is about each person being a leader because each individual is responsible for his or her own territory. Therefore, managers are looking for candidates with leadership experience.

What Not to Do: There is absolutely no excuse for not being able to provide an example of leadership. Examples could be drawn from activities related to church, school, sports, careers, community volunteerism, and so on.

Your Plan: Include a leadership experience in STAR format, choosing one that requires activities similar to those of a pharma rep. Notice that the italicized words in the following example relate to pharma job duties.

Great Answer: "In my last position, I was selected from twenty other human resource representatives to administer our company's insurance education programs. This involved handling all the administrative aspects of signing employees up for courses, distributing study materials, and testing employees. However, the most important role was *"selling"* the coursework to our employees and encouraging them to *enhance and extend their insurance knowledge.* To do so, I *focused on the benefits* to the employees of obtaining advanced insurance certifications. For example, I *emphasized how* advanced certifications usually result in more promotions and higher salaries and also increase employees' marketability for future jobs inside or outside the company. I also *implemented a rewards program* for passing exams and gaining certifications. Many of the rewards became so coveted by employees that they took the courses simply for the rewards they offered. Regardless of the employee's intentions, the company's Human Resource VP attributed higher employee retention largely to my successful programs. In my first year in this leadership role, we had a 30 percent increase in students, and by the second year it was an increase of 60 percent. Equally important was the fact that the marketing department attributed its increased efficiency to the increasing number of reps taking the courses. In effect, our marketing reps were better able to handle agent inquiries and problems due to the advanced knowledge they obtained through these courses."

Your Response: _____

_____

_____

_____

_____

33. How competitive are you? Rate yourself on a scale of 1 to 10.

What They're Trying to Determine: Obviously, if you're not competitive, this is not the job for you. So, how high do you rate yourself? And can you back up your rating with an example that illustrates why you chose that number?

What Not to Do: Any rating lower than a 7 is not good. This is no time to be humble.

Your Plan: Using your brag book, illustrate how competitive you are by showing excellent sales numbers and other data, referrals from customers or clients, letters of recommendation, company awards, bonus checks, exceptional grades, and so on. Also, make sure you mention that you enjoy being part of a team. The manager may have had bad experiences with "mavericks", so be sure to focus part of your answer on teamwork.

Great Answer: "I would say that I'm a 10 as far as being competitive. I push myself to be the best, regardless of the competition. I definitely have an intrinsic motivation to be number one in whatever I do. This extends to my career and to other parts of my life as well. In graduate school, I was determined to get a 4.0 GPA. I worked hard, and because of my tenacity, I persevered. Most of my courses were highly technical in nature and graded on a curve, so the competition was fierce. Because I had set that goal, I was determined to achieve it. Although it was difficult because I also carried a full-time job, I maintained a 4.0 GPA throughout grad school. *(Show brag book transcripts.)* However, just because I'm a fierce competitor doesn't mean I'm unaware of the importance of working with team members to achieve a shared goal. I do that with determination as well. I love the challenge of learning new things every day. That's why I will always value the advice of management, partners, or other team members. I feel confident enough to share my successful strategies with partners and coworkers, and I know that in a team environment, their success is my success. I am usually the motivating force behind a team's success. Because I'm so competitive, I strive to be number one on a personal level and on a team level, as well."

Your Response: _____

_____

_____

_____

_____

Interview Questions and GREAT Answers that Showcase Your Qualifications and Fit for Pharmaceutical Sales

34. What is your current occupation?

What They're Trying to Determine: How do the required skills and duties in your current position relate to those needed in pharmaceutical sales jobs?

What Not to Do: Failing to align your present position's required skills, abilities, and duties to those needed in pharmaceutical sales is a big, big mistake.

Your Plan/Great Answer: Very simply, your mission is to highlight the aspects of your current and previous positions that directly relate to pharmaceutical sales. Does your job include these skills? Determine which skills are required in your present job, and then provide an example of how you would utilize each of those skills to successfully perform the duties of a pharmaceutical sales rep. Here are some possible examples:

- Understanding and presenting technical information in an easy-to-understand manner
- Negotiating, persuading, selling, relationship selling, solution selling
- Good listening and communication skills
- Ability to analyze needs and provide solutions
- Presentation skills
- Rapport building
- Tenacity and determination
- Minimal need for supervision
- Outside sales, teaching experience
- Problem solving
- Extensive product knowledge

Your Response: _____

_____

_____

_____

_____

35. What kind of rating did you receive on your last performance appraisal?

What They're Trying to Determine: How does your performance rate in relation to the goals and objectives established in your current position? Regardless of your position, do you strive to be the best at whatever you do? Are you a strong performer, and do you constantly push yourself to be better and do more?

What Not to Do: Don't concentrate on problem areas or areas with low scores. Highlight those exceptional areas *(skills/abilities/duties)* that relate directly to pharmaceutical sales.

Your Plan: Highlight the skills, qualities, and experiences *(those that relate specifically to pharma sales)* for which you've received high ratings, and provide examples that demonstrate why you received those high marks. *(You should have your last couple of performance appraisals in your brag book.)*

Great Answer: "I've consistently received high ratings in my teaching job. In all of my performance appraisals, my principal has noted that I have *garnered the respect* of students, teachers, administrators, and parents. I believe this is due to always being *honest* and operating my classroom with *integrity and respect.* In addition, I constantly *encourage students' questions, employ active listening skills to determine their needs,* and then *design* lesson plans *based upon the information gained.* Teaching biology, I have to be *able to present information to my students in an easy-to-understand manner.* My most recent performance appraisal stated that my *presentation skills* were exceptional as was my *ability to bring the information 'down or up to the level of the listener'.* My *desire for continuous improvement* has always been noted in my performance appraisals, as has my *willingness to share* novel teaching strategies. Administrators often remark that my high energy and *enthusiasm is a great sales tool,* as it encourages students to *buy into* the information I'm presenting. In fact, here's a copy of my last performance appraisal *(show brag book)." (Notice how many of the skills in this answer relate to pharmaceutical sales duties.)*

Your Response: _____

_____

_____

_____

_____

YOU MIGHT WANT TO KNOW:

What is a Brag Book, and how do I make one?

What is a brag book?

A brag book is a must have for any face-to-face pharmaceutical sales interview.

If you want to stand out from the competition and add credibility to the claims you make in your résumé, you should spend a little time putting a brag book together.

A brag book is a sales aid, and no true salesperson should interview without one. Just as salespeople rely on a sales aid to sell the features and benefits of their service or product, you should have a brag book to sell yourself to your interviewer.

What is the purpose of a brag book?

A brag book, if well constructed and used properly in an interview, can add life and credibility to your résumé. It can also help your interviewer remember details about you when the interview day is done.

What do I include in my brag book?

Take a look at your résumé. Make a list of all of your accomplishments, and then think about how you can document them in your brag book You want to include tangible evidence of as many achievements as possible. For some, this may be an easy task. For those of us who tend not to save everything, it may take some digging and a few phone calls to get this written information.

Some ideas of what to include in your brag book:

- Notes from company personnel congratulating you on your most recent sales award
- Copy of the front of a wall plaque that documents your sales achievements, if you have received one
- Performance reviews
- Ranking reports that show your performance
- For recent college grads, a college transcript (if your GPA was 3.0 or higher)
- Letters of recommendation from previous employers, professors, and so on
- Certificates of completion of any special courses you have taken
- Photos of you accepting awards

- Pay stub that shows your outstanding commissions with a previous employer
- Documented achievements that show your leadership skills or positions held
- Business card that shows your previous job title
- President's Club status notification
- Photos of yourself at the President's Club trip

How do I assemble my brag book?

After collecting your documentation, take note of how many pages you have. Go to a local office supply store and purchase a sales binder with clear plastic insert pages (a.k.a. a "pitch book"). Pitch books are sold with varying numbers of pages, so choose the size that best accommodates the quantity of your documents.

Before putting your pages into the book, highlight the main points on each page in yellow marker. Assemble the contents in reverse chronological order, with the most recent first. You may also want to tab your pages for quick access if you have a lot of information.

How do I use my brag book?

When a question about your accomplishments or achievements comes up in your interview, answer the question, and then refer to the sections of the brag book that back up your claims. Use a pencil to point to the highlighted points (you don't want the interviewer to have to read all of the information).

Practice using your brag book, and remember where your information is located within the pages. The last thing that you want to do is fumble around looking for the information. Also, keep in mind that it is not necessary to show all your information. Play it by ear; if the interviewer is truly interested in seeing it all, by all means, brag away! If the interviewer seems uninterested, don't continually refer to the book. The brag book is meant to support your verbal answers to questions, not actually to be those answers.

Ideas of what to include in my brag book:

1. _____

2. _____

3. _____

4. _____

5. _____

6. _____

7. _____

8. _____

9. _____

10. _____

36. What is your greatest weakness?

What They're Trying to Determine: Do you have enough self-awareness to recognize weaknesses and to work to overcome them whenever possible? Your willingness to better yourself, personally and professionally, is a sign of maturity.

What Not to Do: Stating "I really can't think of anything, right now" is a big mistake. Such a response leads the interviewer not to view you as an honest person and not to believe that you are a goal-oriented, determined, or motivated worker. Also, do not say something like, "Well, I'm not a paperwork person." This response basically screams, "Hey, I'm not a 'detail person,' so get over it!" and isn't a good response, either. Even though your primary duty will be sales, you will still need to push papers to some extent. Guess what? Organizational skills are a key component of pharmaceutical sales jobs, so don't dismiss them as unimportant.

Your Plan/Great Answer: In crafting your response, think of a "weakness" that is fairly harmless—one that could possibly be considered a positive trait. For example, you could say, "I'm a bit of a workaholic; I'm often so focused on my goals that I develop tunnel vision …" Next, tell how you've worked to overcome the "weakness". Continuing on from the response above, you might say, "But I've learned how to better organize my time as well as to create more realistic short- and long-term goals." The next step is to provide an example of how you've experienced professional success as a result of working to overcome your weakness. "As a result, I've become much more efficient and effective in reaching both professional and personal goals. For example,

I recently finished a successful project well within deadline but also had extra time—because of my new organization system—to train for a marathon and return to graduate school." An example such as this shows that you are a creative problem solver. You've turned a negative into a positive! Finally, indicate that you still struggle with your weakness from time to time. *Note:* If you state that you've overcome this weakness completely, then it's no longer a weakness. As a result, the manager could request that you describe a current weakness. You don't want *that* to happen, do you? Then do as we say, and you'll only have to answer the question once!

Your Response: _____

_____

_____

_____

_____

37. Tell me about a time when you had to make a quick decision. What was the result?

What They're Trying to Determine: Can you think on your feet? Are you a fast thinker? Pharma reps constantly have to make decisions when faced with a variety of unforeseen situations in their territory. Will you be able to act quickly and come up with positive solutions to problems?

What Not to Do: Don't give an example of a time when you had to choose between french fries and mashed potatoes.

Your Plan/Great Answer: Make sure that your answer clearly demonstrates the ability to think quickly and produce favorable results. Provide the answer in STAR format, and make sure that the result is powerful. Also, relate something of the process you used in making your decision. What specific factors influenced you to make the decision you did? Then link your decision-making process to how a pharma rep often must think on his or her feet. When a doctor is not available to speak with a rep, for instance, a decision must be made. Does he or she wait or go on to the next clinic?

Your Response:

S_____

_____

T_____

_____

A_____

_____

R_____

_____

38. Tell me which pharmaceutical sales duty you'd like the least?

What They're Trying to Determine: Is the aspect you'd like the least an important part of pharmaceutical sales? If it is, this career is probably not a good match for you. Also, this question seeks to reveal your knowledge of the job. Do you know the essential duties well enough to even answer this question?

What Not to Do: If you don't pick at least one aspect, it will seem that you are ungenuine and unrealistic.

Your Plan: Pick a fairly unimportant duty to comment on as your "least" favorable aspect of pharmaceutical sales. But don't stop there... turn it into a positive for you.

Great Answer: "At first glance, I would say the least favorite part of this job for me might be the large amount of "wait time" in clinics—waiting to speak with prescribers. Because I'm so energetic and motivated to get out there and speak with physicians, this could be difficult for me. After careful thought, however, I've come up with a number of ways to further my skills during my wait time. For example, I could use it as an opportunity to increase my product knowledge by reading recent studies or journal articles. That would make me a more effective consultant to my prescribers. Also, I could use the time to build my relationships with the gatekeeper and other office staff, which is important to the success of my products as well."

Your Response: _____

_____

_____

_____

_____

YOU MIGHT LIKE TO KNOW:

Successful pharmaceutical sales representatives are almost religious in their enthusiasm for their work. If challenges, competition, and hard work give you a rush, you will love this job!

39. Why do you wish to leave your current career?

What They're Trying to Determine: This question is often used to incur a slew of negative responses. Any negative responses during the interview process can quickly put an end to your chances of progressing further. Of course, the interviewer is also interested in why you are choosing to enter pharma sales.

What Not to Do: Don't blast your current manager or colleagues, or even your company in general.

Your Plan/Great Answer: State matter-of-factly that you wish to work in a career that has upward mobility, a great deal of challenge, and rewards for a job well done. Also, if applicable, you can say that you've risen to the top of your department, overcome many challenges, and are now ready for a new challenge. You also feel that it is important to you that your career makes a difference in the world. The pharma sales profession benefits society by extending and enhancing people's lives. Additionally, you may choose to mention how recession proof the industry is, due to the large population of baby boomers nearing retirement and the fact that as long as disease and sickness exist there will be a need for pharmaceuticals. Finally, pharmaceutical sales is considered an elite sales job because of its many challenges and rewards. "Because I'm so competitive, I want to be among the best of the best, continuously pushing myself to become a more capable and confident salesperson. A career in pharmaceutical sales will help me do just that."

Your Response: _____

_____

_____

_____

_____

✓ THE BABY BOOMER BOOM
WebMD Medical News:

Baby boomers are now set to revolutionize and revitalize the pharmaceutical industry, much like they did the diaper industry years ago, say antiaging experts speaking at a symposium in New York City.

Born between 1946 and 1964, the 80 million baby boomers change every market they enter, and the pharmaceutical industry will be no different. By 2025, at least 15 percent of all Americans will be older than 65, and people older than 85 are the most rapidly growing segment of the population.

40. What are your current job duties and responsibilities?

What They're Trying to Determine: Similarly to the previous question about your current position, the manager is trying to determine if your current job's skills and duties are similar to those for pharmaceutical sales jobs.

What Not to Do: Many times, candidates list their current job duties without any regard to pharmaceutical sales or otherwise fail to show the link between their current position's responsibilities and those of pharma sales. Don't make that mistake!

Your Plan/Great Answer: Highlight only those skills and duties that transfer directly to pharmaceutical sales jobs, and be sure always to show your sales prowess. Haven't you "sold" someone an idea or persuaded a colleague, friend, or relative to take a certain course of action? Of course you have! Again, describe the links between a pharma sales rep's duties and responsibilities and those of your current position.

Your Response: _____

_____

_____

_____

_____

41. What will your references say about you?

What They're Trying to Determine: Can you be objective about your references? Can you back up your assertions of experience and success with proof from previous managers and colleagues (i.e., your references)?

What Not to Do: "Fluff" responses such as "They'll say I'm a great people person" are not powerful enough to win you the job. *Note:* Never use the term "people person"—managers hate it. Many managers have told me that they grimace when they hear that term. Another reply managers hate to hear is, "I just really like people!" That's an inadequate reason for entering pharma sales.

Your Plan/Great Answer: Be specific and provide proof. Also, make sure you have spoken with your references and that you know exactly what they will say about you. Prior to your interview, provide your references with a list of two or three skills and accompanying examples that prove you possess those skills. Make sure your skills list contains the skills most directly related to pharma sales. For example, "Ted Jones will provide examples of how my communication and negotiation skills helped resolve many customer complaints and actually led to a 30 percent increase in current client sales. Angela Smith will speak of my ability to build great rapport with my clients and to act as a consultant, not just another salesperson. She spoke of that quality in a performance review."

Your Response: _____

_____

_____

_____

_____

42. You've switched jobs several times over the last five years. Can you explain why?

What They're Trying to Determine: Are you a job hopper? If we give you this position, will you be leaving within a year or two, causing us to waste money and time on training?

What Not to Do: Don't get overly defensive or emotional; that would look suspicious and cause doubt in the manager's mind about hiring you. Don't give negative responses about former companies, managers, or colleagues.

Your Plan/Great Answer: Your reasons for leaving each position must be realistic and positive. Each jump should be cast as a move to a more lucrative position or a position with increased responsibilities. You may also want to mention that you switched jobs for a position that required many of the same skills and duties that pharma sales jobs do. Try to link each reason for leaving to a positive aspect of pharmaceutical sales jobs. For instance, "In my former position as a physical therapist, I liked the *consultative relationship* I developed with my patients, but I missed the sales aspect of it. Patients came to me—I didn't have to convince them to buy my services. Because of my *competitive spirit,* I decided to pursue my passion and obtain a more conventional sales position." Notice how the italicized words relate directly to pharmaceutical sales?

Your Response: _____

_____

_____

_____

_____

How does your job experience, both current and former, compare to pharmaceutical sales?

What They're Trying to Determine: Do you have a breadth of experience with skills that are directly transferable to pharmaceutical sales?

What Not to Do: Don't speak of any job responsibilities or duties that do not directly relate to pharmaceutical sales. Focus only on the relevant aspects of your previous positions with regard to the duties of a pharmaceutical sales rep.

Your Plan/Great Answer: Detail your experience in negotiating, persuading, consulting, understanding and presenting technical information, closing clients, providing creative solutions, thinking outside of the box, being responsible for yourself, working in a team environment, and excelling on a consistent basis. Provide brief and specific examples of each of these, based upon previous responsibilities or successes you've experienced in your jobs to date.

Your Response: _____

_____

_____

_____

_____

YOU MIGHT LIKE TO KNOW:

The number one complaint about interviewees is their lack of preparation. An interview is just like a sales call: you're selling yourself to the prospective employer. When it's your turn to talk, say something as simple as "In preparing for this interview, I ..." (and then list what you did). This will show the interviewer that you prepared conscientiously for the interview. Here are some examples:

- "I read your last three corporate reports."
- "I took one of your salespeople to breakfast."
- "I spent an hour on your website to see how I fit into your mission."
- "I had an informational interview with one of your customers about how you sell and service your products."

The point is to talk about your preparation. Sales managers want to know that you're willing to dig for information. If you're not willing to do that to get a job, then why would you be willing to do it to land a sale once on the job?

 Have you interviewed with other pharmaceutical companies?

What They're Trying to Determine: Are other companies interested in you, and if not, why not? If other companies are not currently interviewing you, the manager will wonder if you're really someone worth pursuing.

What Not to Do: Don't be specific, because it is not in your best interest to "tell all." If you divulge too much information, the manager may later use this private information against you. Do not reveal specifically who you're interviewing with. We have personally witnessed managers sabotage their candidate's other opportunities (with competing pharma companies) when armed with this knowledge.

Your Plan: Very simply, your answer should convey the following:

- I am a candidate worth considering.
- I'm interested in your company, first and foremost.
- I'm serious about this career and want to make sure I align myself with the best company for me.

Great Answer: State that you're not taking this career path lightly. For example, "After careful research and consideration, I am exploring my options with a number of pharmaceutical companies. Obviously, I need to make sure that there's a good fit between us before I proceed further in the interview process. Based on what I've found through research online and information from your reps in the field, in addition to what I've witnessed in this interview thus far, I'd say that your company is my first choice because ..." *(Name four or five specific facts you discovered about the company that convinced you it's the right one for you.)*

Your Response: _____

_____

_____

_____

_____

45. What attracted you to the college major you chose?

What They're Trying to Determine: Are your interests and goals aligned with this job? Is your education and experience transferable to pharmaceutical sales?

What Not to Do: Failing to link your college major and pharmaceutical sales in some way limits your chances of moving on to the next step. Managers want to know that your college coursework, in addition to your experience, prepared you for this position.

Your Plan/Great Answer: Show that your college major provided a background that directly relates to pharmaceutical sales jobs. How do you do that? If you were a music major, for instance, bring out the fact that you like creating rapport with your audience; you have presentation skills; and in order to connect with the audience, you have to sell your knowledge of music as well as possess the ability to present your music in an entertaining manner that holds people's attention. You've also been in many plays and musicals. You've enjoyed competing for top parts and the challenge of learning and memorizing a large amount of information in a short amount of time. *(See how it's similar to pharmaceutical sales?)* Rapport building, presentation skills, selling your subject knowledge, dealing with competition, communication skills, and ability to learn and present information—all are essential aspects of pharma sales jobs.

Your Response: _____

_____

_____

_____

_____

46. How do you rank in comparison to others in your same position?

What They're Trying to Determine: Do you have a history of excellence and success? Have you been placed in positions of leadership due to your consistent record of success?

What Not to Do: Failing to provide any sort of benchmark or corroborating statements from managers and colleagues with which to measure your success will make your statements appear questionable and invalid.

Your Plan/Great Answer: In this answer, managers are looking for achievements that can be quantified with numbers and proof. Provide ranking information, performance appraisals, sales data, and client recommendations. If none of this is available, consider presenting statements of recommendation from previous managers or colleagues that refer to your exceptional abilities and prove that you are a standout. Make sure that all this information is in your brag book.

Your Response: _____

_____

_____

_____

_____

HELPFUL HINT FOR USING BENCHMARKS

Whenever possible, use benchmarks to prove your success. Don't just state: "I improved my sales by 20 percent." *(Think of this from a manager's point of view; he or she may be thinking, "So what?")* If you add a benchmark to your answers, you are bound to impress. Let's look at that statement again, this time adding a benchmark. "I increased my sales by 20 percent compared to a company average of 3 percent." *(This is much more impressive, wouldn't you agree?)* Here's another example: Don't just say: "I was the third-best best salesperson in the country." Rather, say: "I was the third-best rep in the country out of 250." *(Do you see how benchmarks can better prove your abilities?)* Use them, and use them often!

Do you currently have to prepare reports or utilize record-keeping software in your position?

What They're Trying to Determine: Do you have basic-level computer skills? Pharmaceutical reps must record pre-call objectives, call details, and post-call analysis. There will also be various projects assigned to your team that will require a fair amount of computer work. In addition, there are numerous online training courses you'll be expected to take on a routine basis. Remember, they're not asking you to be a computer genius … just to possess basic computer abilities.

What Not to Do: Unless you've been living under a rock, you should be able to speak intelligently about this subject. This is not the time or place to say that you and your computer just don't get along.

Your Plan/Great Answer: Provide specific examples of how you utilize the computer for recording data, analyzing data, finding new information, creating solutions, communicating with others, following up, and generating reports. Also, state that you realize the use of computers is a valuable and necessary component of any job, and you feel certain you will be able to learn the company's software systems.

Your Response: _____

_____

_____

_____

_____

48. How do you balance career and family?

What They're Trying to Determine: Can you handle this challenging career in addition to your family responsibilities? Similar to the "how do you handle stress" question, this one aims to elicit information about how you stay organized and in control.

What Not to Do: Don't divulge any information about your family that you don't need to. It would not be helpful, for instance, to state that your child or husband has a behavioral or health issue that takes a lot of your time.

Your Plan/Great Answer: Explain how your great organizational skills set you apart from others. Tell how your daily to-do lists and prioritizing help you maintain a firm grasp of your goals and responsibilities, and the steps to accomplish them, in your career and family life. *(At this point, you may wish to take out your planner or organizer and show your task lists, appointment calendar, and any other organization systems you are using.)* State that you employ stress-management techniques, such as exercising and reading, to de-stress your life. You may also mention additional elements (specifically related to pharmaceutical sales jobs) that help you achieve balance. For example, having a high degree of autonomy in your job and supportive relationships both inside and outside of work helps achieve that balance as well.

Your Response: _____

_____

_____

_____

_____

49. What is your current salary?

What They're Trying to Determine: Should we waste our time interviewing you if your current salary is far beyond what we're prepared to offer a new rep? Surprisingly enough, this is the one question that can eliminate a candidate on the spot. If you are making a substantial salary now and are willing to take a significant pay cut to enter pharmaceutical sales, most managers will need to have a convincing answer as to why.

What Not to Do: Don't say anything that could ruin your chances of landing the job. You don't want the manager to think he or she can't afford you, nor do you want the manager to think you're desperate if you indicate a lower-than-expected salary. Don't disclose information about your current salary, as you may be eliminated before you have the opportunity to sell yourself. Don't discuss specific numbers until you've been formally offered the job. You also don't want to say that you are willing to accept a lower salary to work in a poorly performing territory because you know that you will be able to turn the territory around in no time and then make up for the difference. The reality is that poorly performing territories take work and a lot of time to turn around.

Your Plan /Great Answer: "I've done quite a bit of research on beginning pharmaceutical sales salaries. (You may want to mention only your base salary with your current position.) I have a base salary that is very comparable to that of a pharmaceutical rep. I'd be looking for an opportunity to be within the $45k–$62k base range."

Your Response: _____

_____

_____

_____

_____

How are you evaluated in your current profession?

What They're Trying to Determine: Are you evaluated in a way that is similar to how pharmaceutical sales reps are evaluated? If so, this will show the manager that you are familiar with the expectations and requirements of pharma sales work.

What Not to Do: Don't comment, even if it's true, that there isn't any formal evaluation system in your current position, as it would discredit all your accomplishments in that position.

Your Plan/Great Answer: Show the similarities between how you're currently evaluated and how a pharm rep is evaluated. For example, are you evaluated on your contributions to a team? Do you have to grow a certain percentage of the business or hit a specific number? Are you provided a bonus or higher rankings among peers based on your ability to bring in more money or expand the customer base? Are you evaluated based on how many customer sales calls you average per day? Are you evaluated in terms of your ability to prioritize and focus on the 80/20 rule *(80 percent of your business comes from the top 20 percent of prescribers/ buyers)*? Are you evaluated in terms of your ability to build rapport with your customers and clients? Are you evaluated on your ability to reach or exceed predefined goals set by you and/or your manager? In summary, link the criteria by which you're currently evaluated *(not just on a formal basis but also on an everyday basis)* to the criteria by which pharma reps are evaluated. If you can highlight the similarities between the two jobs' evaluation systems, your status as a good candidate will rise significantly.

Your Response: _____

_____

_____

_____

_____

✔ MORE ABOUT THE 80/20 RULE

Pareto's Principle, the 80/20 rule, should serve as a daily reminder to focus 80 percent of your time and energy on the 20 percent of your work that is really important. Eighty percent of your business will come from 20 percent of your customers. Don't just work smart—work smart on the right things.

---

51. Are you more analytical or more creative?

What They're Trying to Determine: How do you describe yourself? If the manager is more creative than analytical, he or she may wish you to be that way as well, and vice versa. However, most managers believe that pharmaceutical sales jobs require a large portion of both analytical and creative skills.

What Not to Do: Don't paint yourself into a corner; don't choose one characteristic over the other.

Your Plan/Great Answer: "I have a pretty equal amount of analytical and creative skills. Of course, different situations require different skill sets. I have the ability both to analyze complicated situations and data and to create out-of-the-box solutions to problems." *(Next, state an example of a situation in which you utilized both skill sets to create a particular success.)*

Your Response:

S _____

_____

T _____

_____

A _____

_____

R _____

_____

52. What skills do you have that make you qualified to work in pharmaceutical sales?

What They're Trying to Determine: Can you sell yourself into this position? Do you know enough about this career, based upon your knowledge of the required skill sets and experience, to sell yourself?

What Not to Do: Stating that you have great communication skills and sales experience is not enough.

Your Plan/Great Answer:

1. First, make a list of the essential skills and abilities required in pharmaceutical sales jobs.
2. For every skill or quality listed in Step 1, devise a STAR response— a real-life example illustrating how you possess the skill or ability

in the STAR format. Write down and then practice the description of the best example for every skill or quality on your list. Don't forget: you should also point to applicable "proof pages" within your brag book.

3. Rehearse your answers until your delivery is smooth and confident.

At the end of this answer, follow up with a trial close: "Based on the information I've just provided and proven with my brag book, do you believe that I'm qualified to work in pharmaceutical sales and that I'll be a successful rep?" If the manager says "no" or hesitates, ask what areas you could address that would prove your qualifications. Once a "yes" is obtained, utilize that "yes" in your close at the end of the interview. "Earlier you stated that I am qualified to work in pharmaceutical sales and that you believe I will make a successful rep. That having been said, may I gain a commitment from you that I will be asked back for another interview?" *(Smooth, very smooth!)*

Your Response:

Communication Skills: Active Listening/Presentation Skills, Rapport Building

S—situation (background) _____

_____

T—task (problem) _____

_____

A—action (what you did) _____

_____

R—result _____

_____

Organization/Prioritization/Needs Assessment

S _____

_____

T _____

_____

A _____

_____

R_____

_____

Integrity/Honesty/Trustworthiness/Loyalty

S _____

_____

T _____

_____

A _____

_____

R_____

_____

Determination/Tenacity

S _____

_____

T _____

_____

A _____

_____

R_____

_____

Goal-Driven Attitude/Leadership

S _____

_____

T _____

_____

A _____

_____

R_____

_____

Sales Success/Skills: Persuading/Negotiating/Closing

S _____

_____

T _____

_____

A _____

_____

R_____

_____

Problem Solver/Creative Thinker

S _____

_____

T _____

_____

A _____

_____

R_____

_____

Ability to Understand Technical/Difficult Information

S _____

_____

T _____

_____

A _____

_____

R _____

_____

53. How do you feel about paperwork?

What They're Trying to Determine: Can you handle a job that requires a good amount of paperwork for record keeping and reports?

What Not to Do: Don't say that you feel that paperwork is a "necessary evil". You should not mention anything negative related to pharmaceutical sales jobs.

Your Plan/Great Answer: State that paperwork has its uses. It would be difficult to achieve success in any job without record keeping, goal planning, and analysis, all of which requires organized documentation. Mention that you are used to doing paperwork in your current position and that you are very diligent in getting it done on time. *(The biggest pet peeve of many a manager is late or poorly done paperwork. If reports are late getting to managers or are incomplete or inaccurate, the managers in turn cannot complete their work.)*

Your Response:

S _____

_____

T _____

_____

A _____

_____

R _____

_____

54. What is your ability to learn technical information?

What They're Trying to Determine: Can you learn the highly scientific and technical information you need to know to accurately sell our products? What proof do you have that you can learn this information?

What Not to Do: Don't think that this is all about your ability to pass science classes in school.

Your Plan/Great Answer: Utilize a variety of examples to prove your ability to learn and present technical information. Have you come to know your current company's products inside and out, and are you able to speak intelligently about them? Have you learned extensive details and become highly knowledgeable about a particular industry or computer program? Are there particular subject areas that you have learned about through extensive research? In answering this question, consider this: What is your expertise? Also, you should refer to a number of difficult technical courses you took in high school and college, and to the good grades you received in those technical classes, as proof of your ability to learn and synthesize technical information. *(Make sure your transcripts are in your brag book.)*

Your Response: _____

_____

_____

_____

_____

ON A SIDE NOTE

There are some online companies that sell medical technology courses, claiming that if you study their materials, you will have an edge over your competition in interviews. Don't buy or study this material prior to interviewing. You have enough to know going into an interview without also having to learn medical terminology. All of the medical terminology and science that you need to know for selling will be taught in your initial training.

55. In the work environment, would you rather be right or win?

What They're Trying to Determine: Are you concerned more with ethical and knowledgeable behavior or with beating the competition?

What Not to Do: Don't try to pick one preference or the other because you have no idea which the manager prefers.

Your Plan/Great Answer: Provide your own interpretation of the question so that you can choose both aspects. For example, you could say, "Well, if you're defining 'right' by exhibiting ethical and honest behavior and also by making sure that the information I provide is factually correct, then I do strive to be 'right'. But, if you're asking if I always have to be right, then no ... I don't. When you start thinking in that manner, you stop striving to learn and better yourself ... and that would be a big roadblock to success. Because I'm such a competitive person, however, I equally want to win in every goal and task that I pursue. I think that, to be successful, you have to be 'right' in the sense of being honest and behaving ethically in your relationships as well as being knowledgeable about your products.

Your Response: _____

_____

_____

_____

_____

ARE YOU TOO OLD TO BE
A PHARMACEUTICAL SALES REP?

The question that often comes up is this: "I have great outside sales experience, dress well, am very motivated, and keep in-shape. I am 45, but people always tell me that I don't look a day over 30. Do I have a shot at pharma sales? I have heard that they like to hire kids in their 20s.

Answer: Yes, you do. Although it is true that many pharma reps are in their 20s, there are also many reps in their 30s, 40s, and older. If you were to attend a national sales meeting, you would notice that the group in attendance includes people from all age groups. To discriminate against a candidate for his or her age would be breaking the law. If you are older, dress for the times, make a good impression, and you will have as good a shot at the job as anyone.

56. Why should we hire you over another candidate?

What They're Trying to Determine: Can you summarize your skills and abilities and sell yourself?

What Not to Do: Don't answer this question without pointing to proof in your brag book.

Your Plan/Great Answer: Summarize the key skills, abilities, and experience required in pharmaceutical sales jobs. For each skill or ability, provide a brief STAR response to prove that you possess that skill or ability. Follow that up with a statement of how passionate you are about the industry in general and the company in particular. Regarding the company, give three specific reasons, backed up by research. Show your enthusiasm by being passionate when you answer this question. Lean forward in your chair, smile as you give your answer, and let the excitement show in your eyes!

Want another idea? "I have a proven track record in business and education that demonstrates that I've consistently met and exceeded goals. *(Give examples.)* I am a dedicated, determined candidate who does not accept mediocrity in my work. And I care deeply about furthering your mission." *(State the company's mission.)* Immediately close with: "Based on the proof I've just provided, how confident are you that I'll make a successful rep?" If the manager doesn't provide a positive answer or seems unconvinced, probe to uncover the problem areas, and then provide examples as proof that he or she does not need to be concerned with those areas. Ask the "will I make a successful rep" question again, until the manager gives a positive response. Your closing statement can be something like this: "Great. When should I expect your call to set up the next step?"

Your Response: _____

_____

_____

_____

_____

What is selling to you? How would you describe it?

What They're Trying to Determine: Are your ideas about selling aligned with the pharmaceutical sales industry's definition? Do you progress through a series of stages when you sell?

What Not to Do: Don't gloss over this question. It is an important one, especially if you do not have prior sales experience. It's meant to test your sales knowledge.

Your Plan/Great Answer: You must answer by concisely defining your step-by-step selling method. For example: "Selling involves knowing your product inside and out, prioritizing your accounts with the 80/20 rule, incremental goal setting, follow through and post-call analysis, building good rapport with customers, employing active listening techniques to determine customers' needs and wants, positioning your products according to those needs and wants, and following up with "fanatical" customer service that separates your products and services from those of the competition.

Your Response: _____

_____

_____

_____

_____

Interview Questions and GREAT Answers that Showcase Your Pharmaceutical Sales Industry and Pharmaceutical Sales Job Knowledge

58. What are your income expectations for your first year in pharmaceutical sales?

What They're Trying to Determine: Are you realistic and knowledgeable about what a new pharma rep typically makes in the first year?

What Not to Do: Don't pad the figures in hopes of gaining more money. This would actually stop you from proceeding further in the interview process.

Your Plan/Great Answer: State that you've found through research and networking that most first-year reps make between $50k–$85k in total compensation. "Obviously, I'm aware that my compensation depends upon my sales numbers, and that is very motivating to me; I love the challenge associated with that aspect of pharmaceutical sales. In addition, I'm sure that once we've both determined that we're a good fit for each other, we'll be able to engage in a reasonable dialogue about compensation."

Your Response:_____

_____

_____

_____

_____

59. What do you think are the duties and responsibilities of a pharmaceutical rep?

What They're Trying to Determine: Do you know what you're getting yourself in for? Are you aware of the rigorous demands of this job? Are you knowledgeable about the essential duties and responsibilities of this job?

What Not to Do: Don't be flippant about the "awesome" responsibilities of this job. Show respect for the job and all that it entails.

Your Plan/Great Answer: "I believe that a pharmaceutical rep's job consists of strong territory management, developing in-depth product knowledge and effective selling models, working with team members to further the company's mission, establishing a consultative relationship with prescribers, selling the company's products, and representing the company in a professional and ethical manner at all times."

Your Response: _____

_____

_____

_____

_____

60. What part of the job do you think is the greatest challenge to a pharmaceutical rep?

What They're Trying to Determine: Do you know what the biggest challenges inherent in this job are? The last thing the manager wants is for you to work for 30 days and then quit because you didn't realize what this job was all about. Did you know that each new hire in pharmaceutical sales costs the company anywhere from $80,000 to $95,000? This is why hiring managers drill you with these types of interview questions.

What Not to Do: Don't state the challenge without addressing how you would attack it.

Your Plan/Great Answer: "Based upon my research and previous ride-along experience with a pharmaceutical rep, I believe one of the most difficult aspects of the job is gaining access to 'no-see' or 'rep-unfriendly' clinics. Obviously, it takes a creative salesperson to find a way to gain access to those facilities. Some of the creative sales strategies I have successfully employed are ... *(provide examples of previous situations in which you were creative in obtaining a sale).* Another difficult aspect of the job is gaining significant 'face time' with physicians, especially since face time has substantially decreased over the last 10 years. According to some of my Internet research, the amount of time spent with sales reps by the average U.S. physician decreased from 12 minutes to 7 minutes per day. And, each detail with a doctor lasts an average of only 2.5 minutes. Obviously it's difficult to get your product message across in such a short amount of time. That's why I will always pre-plan every physician call. Knowing my goals and how I plan to reach them will help me utilize the face time with the physician in the best possible manner."

Your Response: _____

_____

_____

_____

_____

61. **Pharmaceutical reps are always time-challenged. There's a lot to be done with little time to do it. How would you stay organized and complete projects within deadlines?**

What They're Trying to Determine: Can you handle the organizational demands of this job? And *(as in similar questions)* are you knowledgeable about the key responsibilities of the job?

What Not to Do: Don't brush off this question lightly. Organization is a key skill, and managers want proof that you'll have a plan for putting it into practice upon getting the job.

Your Plan/Great Answer: "Pharmaceutical companies usually provide computers to their reps for business use. Entering my call notes into the computer after each sales call will allow me to detail the important events of the call in an accurate manner. Then when I get home, I'll only need to log in and download the information. I will also spend an hour or so the night before a sales call completing my pre-call planning and loading my vehicle with samples. This will allow me to be the first rep to arrive at many of my prescribers' offices, which will decrease my downtime and keep my sales-calls-per-day average up. The pre-call planning will allow me to be as effective and efficient as possible in incrementally moving my prescribers toward my goals. My file of articles, reprints, and sales pieces will be with me at all times to ensure that I continue to brush up on my product-knowledge whenever downtime in waiting rooms occurs. By doing all of this, I will have the extra time to complete projects on a timely basis. In summary, by being organized on a daily basis and creating good habits, I will be able to take on additional responsibilities, projects, and training as needed, thereby increasing my effectiveness as a rep."

Your Response: _____

_____

_____

_____

_____

YOU MIGHT LIKE TO KNOW ...

Physicians are perhaps the most important players in pharmaceutical sales. They write the prescriptions that determine which drugs will be used by their patients. Influencing the physician is key to pharmaceutical sales. Historically, this was done with large pharmaceutical sales forces. A medium-sized pharmaceutical company might have had a sales force of 1,000 representatives. The largest companies had tens of thousands of representatives. Currently, there are approximately 100,000 pharmaceutical sales reps in the United States pursuing some 120,000 pharmaceutical prescribers. Drug companies spend over $5 billion annually sending representatives to physicians' offices.

62. How will you find the time to stay current in your product and disease-state knowledge?

What They're Trying to Determine: Can you handle the demands of this job and in addition stay on top of your product knowledge—reviewing old information and learning new information about your products?

What Not to Do: Don't be vague in your answer; tell exactly what you will do to advance your product knowledge. This will also help show your knowledge of the job.

Your Plan/Great Answer: "Pharmaceutical reps must exhibit a fair amount of flexibility in meeting with prescribers. When forced to wait in a clinic, I will use this to my advantage and brush up on product knowledge through journal articles, company sales pieces, and additional company-provided literature. I will make it a personal objective to be a knowledgeable consultant for my prescribers. I'm also aware that companies offer tapes and compact discs that outline product and selling models in detail. I'll be eager to listen to them while driving in my car. And in speaking with other reps, I've discovered that pharmaceutical companies also offer continuous training in product and disease-state knowledge. I will look forward to advancing my product knowledge in many of these ways."

Your Response: _____

_____

_____

_____

_____

63. What is a realistic number of office calls that a rep can be expected to complete each day?

What They're Trying to Determine: Are you knowledgeable about the expectations of this job?

What Not to Do: Don't state a specific number—by giving a range, you will have a better chance of including the specific number of calls per day that the company requires.

Your Plan/Great Answer: "I would say that the average daily number of calls would be between 8 and 10 calls per day. Obviously I will have days in which I will be able to make clinic appointments, and on those days, I may conduct 12 to 14 calls. And then on other days I may not have quite as many appointments because I will be making more cold calls. But I would expect the average number of calls to be between 8 to 10 calls per day."

Your Response: _____

_____

_____

_____

_____

64. What do you know about managed care? How will you sell in a managed care environment?

What They're Trying to Determine: Managed care formularies are an important, and oftentimes difficult to understand, aspect of the pharmaceutical sales rep's job. Are you aware of the significance of managed care in trying to sell your products to prescribers?

What Not to Do: Not knowing about managed care and formularies is not the end of the world, but if you are able to answer this question intelligently, you can easily jump ahead of the other candidates. They won't have a clue about it because they weren't as smart as you were in buying this book!

Your Plan/Great Answer: "As I understand from my research, managed care companies create formularies to indicate which drugs are covered through insurance and in what amounts. A formulary is a select list of brand-name and generic drugs that have been found to offer a clinical or economic advantage when compared to other similar drugs for the same medical conditions. Formularies are commonly used by health maintenance organizations and health insurance companies to help ensure safe, cost-effective health care. They are usually organized in tiers, where Tier I includes generics, Tier II includes preferred branded medications, and Tier III includes branded medications that are somewhat more costly for the patient. Selected covered drugs (thru co-insurance or co-payment) may also be subject to dispensing limits, prior authorization, step therapy, or dose optimization requirements. Knowledge of various managed care formularies and where my products fit within the tiers is important in selling and positioning the products when detailing my prescribers."

65. Describe "lunch and learn" and "in-service" programs. How are they utilized to the company's benefit?

What They're Trying to Determine: How can you best leverage your time with prescribers?

What Not to Do: Don't leave out the details provided in the Great Answer below. It is imperative that you show the manager that you know what these programs and lunches accomplish and how to utilize them to your advantage.

Your Plan/Great Answer:

Lunch and learns. "At least once a week, I will schedule a lunch and learn for a specific medical office. This is probably the best opportunity to get quality face-to-face time with the physicians, because most feel somewhat obligated to give you quality time in exchange for feeding their office staff. This can be a great time to dive into what makes my physicians tick. At the end of my detail presentation, I will ask them to commit to a specific action—perhaps writing three new prescriptions for a specific patient population or agreeing to talk with me further about a specific point.

"Lunch and learns are also a great opportunity to build relationships with the office staff, who are usually more than happy to answer questions about the doctors. In addition, they may provide information or reasoning about their physicians' prescribing habits that I may not have had the opportunity to discover myself. I will pick the office staff members' brains every time I get the chance; it will help build relationships … and we all know that selling is primarily about relationships!"

Don't forget to mention the importance of working with your teammates to make the best use of the company's lunch-and-learn budget. Also, you will want to note that you are aware of the possibility of co-promotion products with other companies, if that applies to your situation. This shows the interviewer that you are knowledgeable about working with other companies to promote a shared drug, and how sharing lunches and resources can maximize your efforts to gain more business from physicians.

Dinner or speaker programs. Pharmaceutical sales companies allocate specific dollars to bringing in trained speakers. These speakers are physicians who have actually been trained by the pharmaceutical company. The speaker program usually occurs at a restaurant, and the trained speaker delivers a presentation about your specific drug.

The speaker programs are not only a great opportunity for your physicians to get important clinical data on your drug—they also set up a great opportunity for dialogue between you and your physicians. It is critical that you build close relationships with your doctors as soon as possible. The more they like and trust you, the more likely they will be to attend your speaker programs. During the program, you can leverage the positive opinions of influential doctors (opinion leaders) with other prescribers who have not yet bought in.

Your Response: _____

_____

_____

_____

_____

BEWARE OF THE HAPPY-GO-LUCKY INTERVIEWER

If an interviewer seems overly friendly or jovial, you may feel that the interview is going so well that you can let your guard down. Don't let this happen. It's true that you want to establish a feeling of camaraderie, but be sure not to reveal things about yourself that are so honest they could actually hurt your chances. The following are three things *not* to say, even if your interviewer is your instant best friend:

1. One of the reasons that I am pursuing a career in pharma sales is that I want a job that is a bit less taxing, hours-wise.
2. I have visions of retiring in the next five years.
3. My wife is interviewing for a job in Washington. I don't think she'll get it, but if she does, it could affect the amount of time I will be staying in this area.

You don't have any experience in sales. How do you plan on learning what you need to know to be successful in selling?

What they're trying to determine: Can you sell if given the opportunity?

What Not to Do: Don't tell the interviewer that you will learn all that you need to know in initial training.

Your Plan: If you don't have sales experience, it is essential that you convince the interviewer that you have an understanding of the sales process. Demonstrate that you have what it takes to make it in sales (communication skills, leadership skills, and rapport-building skills). Explain that all you need is the opportunity to prove yourself and that, given the chance, you know you will excel. Tell the interviewer that you know sales are based not only on the ability to persuade but also on gaining trust and building rapport. You may want to give an example of a time when you were able to persuade someone about something, or perhaps cite the fact that you are great at building and maintaining relationships with customers.

Great Answer: "Although I do not have sales experience, I am quick to learn new tasks and have a good understanding of what it takes to be successful when selling pharmaceuticals. I have the personality to sell successfully and the ability to build long-lasting relationships with office staff and physicians. I am personable, enthusiastic, and creative—important personality traits for making it in sales. I cannot wait to show you what I am capable of."

Your Response: _____

_____

_____

_____

_____

67. When is it legal to trade samples with a rep from another company?

What They're Trying to Determine: How much do you know about the legalities of working in this industry? Do you understand that drugs are subject to tight regulations?

What Not to Do: Don't be vague; be specific about what you can and cannot do with samples.

Your Plan/Great Answer: "It is never legal to trade samples with a rep from another company. Every company has specific and tight record-keeping guidelines regarding the counting and sampling of products. All samples must be accounted for at all times and may be left only for physicians."

Your Response: _____

_____

_____

_____

_____

68. Define a "sample drop". Is it considered a "sales call" in this industry?

What They're Trying to Determine: Do you know the difference between sample drops and sales calls?

What Not to Do: Don't rely on what you've heard about the industry in answering this question. Simply follow the plan stated below.

Your Plan/Great Answer: "No, a sample drop is not considered a sales call. A sample drop is simply leaving your samples at an office and waiting for the prescriber to sign for the samples. As the sample pad is signed, a good rep will take the opportunity to engage in some kind of dialogue with the prescriber to possibly move the conversation into a detail or to build rapport for later sales calls. During a sales call, on the other hand, you take the opportunity to question the prescriber regarding patient needs, provide at least one feature and benefit of your products as related to the prescriber's patients and practice, and gain a commitment to move to the next step."

Your Response: _____

_____

_____

_____

_____

69. **How do pharmaceutical reps interact with physicians? Do they sell, or do they educate? The newest selling environment is oriented more toward education than toward selling. How do reps do this?**

What They're Trying to Determine: Have you researched the pharmaceutical sales industry, and are you aware of the most current sales models and ideologies?

What Not to Do: Don't speak about educating only … selling skills are still required as well, regardless of this shift.

Your Plan/Great Answer: "To partner with physicians and develop good working relationships, I must always educate the physician by providing useful, accurate, and important information—features, benefits, drug interactions, side effects, and applicable patient profiles—to the physician during every call. How can I accomplish this every time? Through pre-call planning that incrementally moves the physician toward our goal. When the physician begins to trust that I always provide useful information in a concise manner, he or she will be more willing to meet with and listen to me. Also, if I provide supporting clinical study data from trusted medical journals, the physician will learn to view me as a consultative partner, because I'm backing up my claims with a credible source. In summary, a rep in today's industry must utilize selling skills to sell the features and benefits of his or her products but must also serve as an educator in providing accurate and important product knowledge backed up by credible sources. This is why it is extremely important that I continue to build my product knowledge and stay up to date with the most current information about my products."

Your Response: _____

_____

_____

_____

_____

70. How do you think the recent lawsuits against pharmaceutical companies have affected the pharmaceutical industry's current selling environment?

What They're Trying to Determine: Are you current in your knowledge about the industry, and have you thought about the possible difficulties you may encounter in this job as a result of the lawsuits?

What Not to Do: Don't focus on the lawsuits or the negative press; the interviewing manager could be trying to trick you into being negative.

Your Plan/Great Answer: "I think it is important now, more than ever, to act as a consultant and partner to physicians by presenting and educating them with accurate and important product information. Reps must also provide a variety of credible sources to back up the claims they make to physicians. The lawsuits have created a greater need for reps who are willing to learn their products and disease states backward and forward. Reps must focus on being consultants to physicians and be viewed as a benefit to physicians' patients, rather than just as salespeople. I think the current environment has also put more responsibility on the shoulders of physicians and reps to report previously unidentified side effects to the pharmaceutical companys' medical departments and MSLs (medical science liaisons) to avoid similar circumstances in the future."

Your Response: _____

_____

_____

_____

_____

DOES YOUR RÉSUMÉ HAVE AN OBJECTIVE?

A clearly stated objective is a must for all résumés. If your résumé doesn't have one, add it just below the header. A pharma sales objective shows hiring managers that you are looking for a pharma sales position—it doesn't leave them guessing. Indicate outright that you want a pharma sales position, and use the body of the résumé to tell them why they should hire you.

71. How do you gain quality time with a physician?

What They're Trying to Determine: Do you know how to build relationships with physicians (the key to success as a pharma rep)?

What Not to Do: Don't simply state the obvious, but also try to demonstrate that you're an "out of the box" thinker.

Your Plan/Great Answer: "First I would make sure to comply with all the PhRMA code rules. *(For information about the PhRMA code, refer to the associated newsletter page on Anne's website: www.pharmaceutical-rep.com.)* Then I would employ active listening skills to discover the physician's rules for contacting him or her, if such rules exist. Otherwise, I would try any of the following methods:

- Leveraging referrals from his mentors or other well-respected thought leaders in the community
- Developing great relationships with the physician's staff and the gatekeeper, in particular

- Lunch and learn/in-service programs
- Speaker programs (for dinner or lunch)
- Hospital displays
- Medical education meetings
- Journal club meetings
- Golf course, basketball games, political rallies—according to the interests of the physician
- Educational programs for the physician's patients at his or her office
- Creating novel ways to gain time with the physician, focusing on hot buttons

For example, if I knew that the physician was particularly interested in a new treatment method, even if it is unrelated to my product, I might find a current research article referencing it and leave it for him or her. Once I've taken the initiative to do that type of thing over and over again, the physician will realize that his or her interests are important to me, which is a great rapport builder. We all like to speak with people who share the same interests as we do. By building good rapport and showing the physician that his or her interests are important to me, I will establish a relationship with the physician, built upon mutual interest. Once that relationship is established, I'll be able to gain more quality time with the physician and eventually build upon that trust to leverage my product."

Your Response: _____

_____

_____

_____

_____

How do you uncover a physician's prescribing habits?

What They're Trying to Determine: Do you have any idea of how to obtain this important information? This is another question designed to determine how much you know about the job of a pharma rep. If you show that you know some about this, it's a feather in your cap.

What Not to Do: Act thoughtful when you say this, like you're thinking of it right then ... even though you already know what you're going to say.

Your Plan/Great Answer: "The best way to determine this is to be an active listener—listening to what the physician says to get clues as to his or her prescribing habits and the features/benefits he or she bases prescribing decisions on. To further determine preferences, I would ask probing questions about the physician's patient population and what class of drugs he or she uses to treat different disease states. In addition, pharmacists and other medical personnel, such as charge nurses and physician's assistants, would be able to provide me with insight into the physician's prescribing habits. Finally, I would access key company reports to verify and add to the information I've already discovered."

Your Response: _____

_____

_____

_____

_____

LEAVE A LASTING IMPRESSION

You should consider leaving a token of yourself after your interview. Leave a pencil behind with a note attached saying, "Call Joe Smith. He's the sharpest one for the job!" And leave your phone number behind. That's what pharmaceutical reps typically do in a doctor's office. So, it's a nice tie-in to what you would do on the job, and it leaves a lasting impression.

Former job candidate Barbara Carlson took this advice. She had no sales experience and was going up against about thirty other candidates. "I really needed to make an impression," she said. "At the end of the interview, I gave the manager a small candle with a note attached. It said, 'I can't wait to IGNITE sales in your district. I am looking forward to joining your sales team.' I signed my name. It worked! I landed the next interview and the job."

73. Once hired, you'll be provided with your territory's physician list and sales data that analyzes the prescribing habits of those physicians. How will you organize and prioritize that information?

What They're Trying to Determine: Do you know how to organize, prioritize, and act in a purposeful manner when provided with information and little supervision or direction?

What Not to Do: Don't state that you'll wait for your manager or partner to help you. You need to appear confident and show that you'll act like a leader.

Your Plan/Great Answer: "I'll organize the information using the 80/20 rule *(discussed in Question 50 and the feature following it)* and prioritize the top 20 percent of prescribers who actually account for 80 percent of my business. These are accounts that I most need to maintain and continue to develop. Next, I'll look at the physicians' potential—that is, I'll determine which physicians potentially could write a large volume of prescriptions for my class of product but are not currently doing so. These physicians will be my next prime targets. Of course, I'll then prioritize the remaining physicians: medium-volume writers who do or do not write for my product, and so on. Basically, I will go through the list, organize it by levels of priority, and set goals based on current writing volume and potential. Obviously, I'd also determine how often I will call on each physician, based on the level of priority I have set for him or her. By analyzing and prioritizing, I will achieve results in the shortest time possible."

Your Response: _____

_____

_____

_____

_____

74. What is co-promotion or team selling, and how does it benefit the pharmaceutical company?

What They're Trying to Determine: How much do you know about this industry and the various selling techniques we use?

What Not to Do: Being ignorant of the key terms utilized in pharmaceutical sales jobs shows a lack of interest. So learn the terms!

Your Plan/Great Answer: "Co-promotion is a sales method in which two companies' sales forces work together to promote the same drug. The companies share expenses (lunches, speaker programs, and so on) and resources (access to journal articles, research, influential physicians trained by the companies, and so on). In this way, efforts to gain more business from physicians are maximized. Not only do you share expenses and resources, but you can also increase your call frequency because of the additional sales reps available to sell the product. (If you know that this particular company utilizes this method with another company, reference the relationship and the product being co-promoted.) Most pharma sales forces are set up to use team selling. You may have others on your team or a specific partner who co-promotes the same products as you do. Again, this maximizes efforts to gain more business with increased call frequency and additional access to resources."

Your Response: _____

_____

_____

_____

_____

75. What aspects of pharmaceutical sales are most vital to success?

What They're Trying to Determine: Do you have the ability to prioritize and anticipate what is most important to success in this job?

What Not to Do: This is not the time to discuss salary, benefits, or compensation as being essential to success.

Your Plan/Great Answer: "I firmly believe that if a candidate has the following skills, he or she will be a successful rep: exceptional active listening skills to determine physicians' and patients' wants and needs; ability to master and present technical information; willingness to become an expert in product and disease-state knowledge; ability to build rapport and trusting relationships with physicians and to sell the whole office on you, as a person, as well as your product; ability to probe to determine writing habits; ability to effectively position a product to meet the needs and wants of the physician and his or her patients; and ability always to gain a commitment to advance the sale. Now, would you like me to provide several examples as proof that I have the specific skills and abilities needed to become a successful rep?" *(If so, provide STAR examples that directly prove you have each of these skill sets and abilities.)*

Your Response: _____

_____

_____

_____

_____

76. How do you plan to increase sales? How long do you estimate that it will take you to make an impact on sales in your territory?

What They're Trying to Determine: Do you have a specific plan to increase sales? Do you have an idea of what it takes to make it in this business?

Your Plan: You need to answer in a way that shows your motivation and dedication to increasing sales.

Great Answer: "Initially, my goal would be to excel in sales training and product knowledge. Being well prepared and knowledgeable out of the gate is a great start. From there, I would get organized and learn my territory. I will use sales data to find potential prescribers and focus on those customers with the most potential. Once I locate them, I will do everything possible to find out what makes them tick. I want to know why they prescribe what they prescribe. If they won't see me, I will work every avenue to see them. I will try them before office hours, after office hours, at the hospital—whatever it takes. I know that the best way to increase sales is to get the message to the doctors and to remind them as often as possible. I realize that building a territory takes time. Relationships need to be built. I'm not looking to increase sales in an unrealistic amount of time. I am here for the long haul. I know that doctors don't change their prescribing habits overnight. I think that the key to increasing sales is being well prepared, working hard at seeing customers, and getting to know customers and their prescribing habits over time. Once I gain their trust, I can gain their commitment. Increasing sales doesn't just happen; it takes time, a great plan of action, and dedication. Eventually, hard work pays off."

Interview Questions and GREAT Answers that Showcase Your Company Knowledge (Three Words of Advice: DO YOUR HOMEWORK)

77. Why do you want to work for our company?

Your Plan/Great Answer: This answer should be based *only* on the research you've done. This answer is not meant to reflect on you; it should be centered solely on the company. Managers will be looking for you to answer in a way that proves that you've done your homework. Come up with three or so positive points that relate specifically to the company (not to pharma sales in general).

Point #1 _____

Point #2 _____

Point #3 _____

78. What do you expect from our company?

Great Answer: "I expect that I will be trained in product knowledge, disease-state knowledge, and the particular selling models the company subscribes to. I expect that I will be rewarded when performing exceptionally and supported when in need of assistance for situations beyond my control. I expect the company to constantly strive to further its mission of enhancing and extending people's lives and *(state something from their mission statement/guiding principles)*. I expect the company to require ethical interactions between reps and physicians by adhering to the PhRMA code. *(Refer to Question 83 for more information about the PhRMA code.)* Finally, I expect the company to provide opportunities for career advancement once I've proven myself to be a leader, sales performer, and team player."

79. What, specifically, can you offer our company?

Great Answer: "I have a competitive spirit, boundless energy, enthusiasm, and a proven history of sales success. I also have a passion for continuous learning that will lead your prescribers to perceive of me as a knowledgeable source of information and a partner that wishes to benefit their patients and their practice. I can also offer my tenacity and determination to always push to the next level of excellence; exceptional listening skills that allow me to determine physicians' needs; integrity, honesty, and professionalism in that I'll always do what I say I'm going to do; and 'outside of the box' thinking." Next, provide examples in STAR format of how you are competitive; have a history of sales success; possess an ability to understand technical information plus a willingness to learn; and are tenacious, determined, and a creative thinker. *(Remember: this doesn't mean you need to have worked in a sales job. Selling is persuading people to buy a product or service, or to buy in to your mode of thinking, or a plan of action.)*

80. Explain diversity.

Great Answer: "Diversity refers to the different backgrounds and experiences people bring with them when working in a team environment. Diversity of race, thinking, experience, skills, behavior, strengths, and learning styles adds to the creativity and purposeful activity of a great company. Such a company responds to its diverse clients through a diverse sales force. Diversity may also refer to a company's line of products—the company tries to diversify into a number of business areas to decrease risk and increase opportunities for profit."

81. Our company is (big pharma or small pharma). Why would you rather work for us than for a (big or small pharma)?

Great Answer if the company is small pharma: "From my research with other reps and online sources, I've come to realize that a small-pharma environment is a better choice for me because its spirit and culture seem to be more entrepreneurial. It also seems to me that small-pharma companies are made up of leaders and self-starters, people who are willing to try things a new way and are not afraid to work hard—all of which my references will say about me. Because you're a small company, you must utilize your sales force and managers efficiently, which basically means no "hand-holding" by managers. I've proven by previous examples *(or give the examples now, if needed)* that I'm a leader and self-starter; I won't need, nor do I desire, any sort of hand-holding. That's why I'm so positive that small pharma is right for me. However, it's not just about the size of the company; it's also about the nature of the company, itself. And, based on the facts that … *(state the two or three most important reasons you wish to work for this company, based upon your research),* I want to work for *this* small pharma company."

Great Answer if the company is big pharma: "From my research with other reps, as well as online information sources, I have come to realize that big pharma is the better choice for me. One of the many reasons I wish to enter this career is the stability associated with the pharma industry. Obviously, big-pharma companies are more stable, due to their diverse array of products. Also, big pharma often has greater access to funds, meaning that a larger amount of money is invested in its own R&D departments. This most often translates into a well-stocked, cutting-edge, and diverse pipeline. In addition, I like the idea of having a number of different career opportunities within the same company. Being able to advance my career in any number of directions within the company is very exciting and motivating to me! I also like the fact that the training provided at big pharma is comprehensive, well utilized, and effective, as proven over time. In addition, with big pharma, there is more name recognition and increased DTC *(direct-to-consumer adver-tising)* spending, both of which help in product promotion—although I certainly won't rely on these advantages. However, it's not just about the size of the company; it's about the nature of the company itself. And, based on the facts that … *(state the two or three most important reasons you wish to work for this company, based upon your research)*, I want to work for *this* big pharma company."

THE PROS AND CONS OF WORKING AT A SMALL PHARMACEUTICAL COMPANY VERSUS ONE OF THE BIGGIES

There are a lot of advantages to working for a small pharmaceutical company. First of all, a small company may be more willing to take a chance on somebody with less experience.

It is easier for you to shine and advance at small pharmaceutical companies. Also, small pharmaceutical companies can become big pharmaceutical companies very rapidly. Small companies may offer stock options as an incentive to stay with them long term. Small companies often get acquired by larger companies, and the original stockholders often get wealthy.

However, working for a small pharmaceutical company is riskier than working for a big one. If your company has a small stable of products, that means it has all its eggs in one basket.

Small pharmaceutical companies don't provide big expense accounts for entertaining clients, and you don't have as much marketing support, either. Also, the territories are bigger, so you have to drive more. Instead of working a territory that's three hours end-to-end, your territory might be an entire state.

Finally, the drugs you'd be selling at a small company may not have the same level of formulary acceptance as those sold by large companies. You could be the best salesperson in world, but if your product is not on formulary with insurance companies, it's going to be tougher to sell.

If you go to work for a small company, you have to be able to handle change really well. There is a huge chance your company will be taken over in the next few years.

82. What do you know about our company? Do we sell proprietary products, or are we licensees of the products? Do we sell only branded products?

Your Plan/Great Answer: Find out about this through research on the company website. "Proprietary products" refers to the fact that the company does its own research and development and has created and tested the product. If the company is a "licensee" of the product, it means that the company did not create or test the product but retains the licenses to it. Basically, licensees have all rights to the drug, including promotion and sales. "Branded products" (as opposed to generic versions of products) are manufactured by the company. A company may utilize a combination of all three strategies—selling some proprietary products, paying other companies for the licensing of some of their products, and selling both branded and generic products.

THE UNADVERTISED JOB MARKET: FOOD FOR THOUGHT

There are currently over 100,000 pharmaceutical reps in the United States, and most of these positions are filled by word of mouth. It is estimated that approximately 75 percent of all openings are never advertised. For information on how to locate unadvertised openings, visit Lisa's website at *www.pharmaceuticalsalesinterviews.com.*

83. What guidelines have been set up to govern pharmaceutical sales reps' interactions with doctors?

Your Plan/Great Answer: "Big pharma" companies generally have signed the PhRMA code; smaller companies may choose not to, however, in order to "level the playing field". These guidelines (referred to as the "pharma code"), which cover pharmaceutical rep/doctor interactions, were originated by the Pharmaceutical Research Manufacturers of America (PhRMA) in 2002. The basic components of this marketing code are as follows:

- *General Interaction:* Interaction should focus on informing the prescriber about scientific and educational information to maximize patient benefits.

- *Entertainment:* Interaction should not include entertainment and should be at a place conducive to providing scientific or educational information. Specifically, this means no "dine and dash", no entertainment, and no recreational events (for example, no sporting events, spa visits, or dancing ladies entertainment … get my drift?).
- *Educational and Health Care Practice–Related Items:* Items may be provided to prescribers, but they should be for the health care benefit of patients and of less than substantial value ($100 or less). Common pharma "leave behinds" include pens, note pads, and inexpensive items relating to patient education. No items may be given for the personal benefit of the physician. In short, nothing should be provided that would interfere with the independence of the physician's prescribing practices.

Interview Questions and GREAT Answers that Showcase and Assess Your Problem Solving Skills and Ability to Generate Creative Solutions

(Remember: Pharmaceutical reps spend most of their time unsupervised and without coworkers. If you want to impress the manager, you will need to prove that you can think on your feet and make smart decisions on your own. Reps that are creative think of ways to make it past the gatekeepers.)

 Describe a problem in your current position that you attempted to solve, but failed.

Suggestions for a Great Answer: This answer should be provided in STAR format. Write down the steps and associated statements on the lines provided under this explanation. Remember, because you do not want to emphasize failure, you should choose a minor problem to talk about—one that wasn't that big of a deal. After finishing the STAR format presentation, explain what you learned from the situation and what you did from then on to guarantee that the "failure" wouldn't happen again.

Your Response:

S _____

_____

T _____

_____

A _____

_____

R _____

_____

What you learned: _____

_____

_____

How it changed your course of action from then on: _____

_____

_____

85. Describe a problem that you overcame.

Suggestions for a Great Answer: This should be a problem that you encountered during your career, but if you can't think of anything career related, you could explain a personal situation … just make sure it's not so personal that it makes the interviewer uncomfortable. This answer should be in STAR format, and it should be a powerful story that shows your problem-solving and out-of-the-box thinking skills.

S _____

_____

T _____

_____

A _____

_____

R_____

_____

86. How have you dealt with a difficult colleague?

Suggestions for a Great Answer: If you haven't had difficulty with a business colleague, think of a college schoolmate, teammate, fellow volunteer, or the like. Make sure the problem was a small-scale one that you no longer feel emotional about. Otherwise, your negative feelings will come through and reflect poorly on your objectivity and ability to think rationally. Also, make sure the resolution was positive and enabled you to work effectively with the colleague to accomplish great things for your company, team, volunteer mission, and so on.

S _____

_____

T _____

_____

A _____

_____

R_____

_____

87. How will you be more successful than the myriad of other reps calling on physicians?

Great Answer: "I'll set myself apart by being an active listener—to discern doctors' hot buttons as well as their prescribing preferences and habits. I'll always be a source of interesting and useful information for doctors, which will benefit both them and the patients in their practice. My willingness to work long hours and become a product and disease-state expert will set my educating/selling methods apart from those of other sales reps. *(Provide an example of a previous position in which you worked long hours, became knowledgeable about a product and industry, and experienced great success.)* I'll also establish great rapport with physicians by consistently showing my interest in their hot buttons and offering to help their patients through patient ed programs whenever possible. Finally, I'll always ask for a commitment … whether it's to talk again or to write three prescriptions in the next week for a specific patient type. I will incrementally move physicians closer to my global goals. *(Provide an example of how you used a sales close to move your customer or client closer to your shared goals.)* I will always represent XYZ pharma in a positive manner, and physicians and office staff will be able to count on my exemplary customer service and follow-through. Frankly, you will not find a more enthusiastic, eager candidate who is more determined to succeed." *(Provide a short explanation of when and how you've succeeded in business due to your enthusiasm and determination.)*

#1
Gain Trust
- Asking good questions
- Being an active listener
- Being a source of interesting & useful information for MDs & patient
- By becoming a product & disease-state expert.
- By always asking for a commitment.

#2
Gain commitment

144

Time + A great plan of action + Dedication = ↑ sales.

88. Describe a sales situation in which you turned a negative into a positive.

Suggestions for a Great Answer: Make sure this situation showcases your persuasion and negotiation skills and your ability to think creatively about a viable solution and then carry it out. Think of your biggest sales success that started with some negative aspect and turned positive because of your ingenious and diligent efforts. Remember ... STAR format!

S _____

_____

T _____

_____

A _____

_____

R _____

_____

BAD CREDIT?

Pharmaceutical companies are known for doing background checks and drug screening prior to making an offer to potential employees. They will also, most often, do a credit check. If you have bad credit, don't lie about it. It's not the end of the world. The worst-case scenario might be that you would not be given a company credit card for your expenses and would be asked to use your own credit card and then get reimbursed.

If you have an appointment scheduled with a physician but he or she isn't ready to speak with you, how long should you wait?

Great Answer: "When a physician's nurse, or the prescriber him- or herself, informs me that the prescriber will not be able to meet at the scheduled time but will meet with me as soon as he or she is caught up with a backlog of patients, it is decision time. Do I stay or do I go? The first factor in deciding how long to wait is whether I have another appointment (directly following this one) to keep and how long it will take to get there. The next factor is how far I've traveled for this appointment. If I've traveled 30 to 50 miles to meet this doctor, I will probably wait as long as it takes … assuming that this is an important doctor in my territory. I may not get another chance to make an impact on this doctor for a long time, so it would make good business sense to wait an hour or so to get face time with this doctor. No matter what the situation is, it is always helpful to consult the doctor's nurse to obtain a realistic picture of how long my wait time may be. He or she may also know whether the prescriber would rather reschedule. It is all about quality time with my doctors. If I wait an hour, and then the doctor is in no mood to talk, it probably would have been better just to reschedule for the next available opening. It's a matter of common sense, based on the criteria I've described, as well as utilizing what I know about this prescriber. My time is valuable, but if this is my big chance to make an impact on a high-volume prescriber (HVP), it might well be worth giving up a couple of calls to move market share with a prescriber who can significantly affect numbers for me and my company."

DRESS TO IMPRESS!

Pharma sales managers like their reps to be immaculate, well dressed, and clean cut. Before interviewing, make sure that your hair has a new trim and your nails are well manicured. If you are a man, you may also want to consider shaving that moustache! Dress your best, choosing something conservative. Dark blue is a favorite among managers. The best advice would be to look presidential.

90. How will you build rapport with your physicians?

What They're Trying to Determine: Do you know how to get people to like you, trust and respect you?

Great Answer: "I will build rapport with my physicians by developing good relations with their office staff—enhancing my relationships with the gatekeeper, the charge nurse, and other key players in the office. I will employ active listening skills to discern the physicians' hot buttons. Once I know what those are, I will build upon them to build positive relationships. People like to talk to others who share their interests, so I will become knowledgeable about my physicians' interests and use them to build a bridge to important discussions about my products. Of course, part of building good relationships with physicians involves serving as a resource. By becoming well-versed in product and disease-state knowledge, I will become an important source of information for my physicians. This will ultimately lead to more detail opportunities and higher-quality relationships with my physicians—relationships built upon trust, respect, and friendship".

91. How will you get more face time with busy physicians?

What They're Trying to Determine: How will you set yourself apart from the other reps?

Great Answer: "I'll set myself apart by being an active listener—to determine doctors' hot buttons as well as their prescribing preferences and habits. I'll always be a source of interesting and useful information for doctors, which will benefit both them and the patients in their practice. My willingness to work long hours and become a product and disease-state expert will set my educating/selling methods apart from those of other sales reps. *(Provide an example of a previous position in which you worked long hours, became knowledgeable about the product and industry, and experienced great success.)* I'll also establish a great rapport with the physician by consistently showing my interest in his or her hot buttons and offering to help his or her patients through patient ed programs whenever possible. Finally, I'll always ask for a commitment. Whether it's a commitment to talk again or to write three prescriptions in the next week for a specific patient type, I will incrementally move the physician closer to my global goals. *(Provide an example of how a sales close moved your customer or client closer to your shared goals.)* I will always represent XYZ Pharma in a positive manner, and physicians and office staff will be able to count on my exemplary customer service and follow-through. Frankly, you will not find a more enthusiastic, eager candidate who is more determined to succeed. *(Provide a short explanation of when and how you've succeeded in business due to your enthusiasm and determination.)* Of course, I'll also set up lunch and learns and speaker programs, go to continuing medical education courses, set up hospital displays, and leverage physicians who are thought leaders and current high prescribers of my products to influence other physicians' prescribing habits."

92. How would you react if, after a visit to the sample closet, you find that a competitor has moved your samples and they can no longer be seen?

Great Answer: "If this happens for the first time, I would simply rearrange the samples and casually mention the situation to the office staff so that if it happens again, it will raise a red flag. If it happens a second time, I would calmly show the staff person in charge of the sample closet what has happened and express my concern from the perspective of the physician and his or her patients. For example, I might say, 'I'd hate for Dr. Johnston to be unable to provide samples for her patients, and looking at the way this sample closet is arranged, it would seem that you only have samples for one drug.' Then I would ask, 'Is there anything I could do to make sure this doesn't happen again and ensure that everyone gets equal space on the shelf?'"

USING KEYWORDS IN YOUR RÉSUMÉ

The key to getting your résumé noticed is to load it with as many pharmaceutical sales–related keywords as possible. This is particularly true when you are applying online. Look at the job listing, and use it to find the keywords. Chances are good that the keywords used by the HR rep to search the database will be right there in the job description. Including even two or three more relevant keywords than your competition—which could be hundreds of people—can make the difference between success and failure in securing an interview.

93. How will you turn gatekeepers into advocates?

Great Answer: "I will turn gatekeepers into advocates by selling the whole office on my product and on myself from the moment I step into the office. How? By respecting their time and offering to come back when their office is not so busy. In addition, I will treat them with respect and make it clear that I value what they have to say. Remembering their names and personal things about them ('Is your daughter feeling better? I know you said she had the flu last week.') or knowing that they like a particular type of chocolate and surprising them with it—will make them feel valued and respected. Asking their opinions about office protocol and physician likes and dislikes will make them feel that they're a valuable source of information to me. Everyone likes to feel valued and important, right?"

94. How would you deal with an irate physician whose misplaced anger lands on you?

Great Answer: "The most important thing is that I wouldn't take it personally. Physicians have bad days, just like we all do. Recognizing and affirming this can deflate the situation. Showing empathy toward the physician—suggesting, for example, that I'd be happy to come back at a time that would be more convenient—will show him or her that I'm more interested in being helpful than in pressing the sale at that time."

95. What will you do when you're told by gatekeepers that their physicians are "no see", meaning that they don't speak with reps?

Great Answer: "There are several methods I could utilize, but the most important thing I can do is gain the respect of the staff first and then utilize the staff to help me forge a relationship with the physician.

Other methods include:

- Having other, respected physicians recommend my products to the "no see" physician.
- Depending on the physician's practice, utilize my good relationship with the specialist to whom he or she refers or to the general practitioner that refers patients to him or her. I'll ask the physician with whom I have a good relationship to intervene and recommend me as someone who can provide useful information and good products.
- Inviting the physician to a speaker program and utilizing a well-respected speaker to influence him or her. If the thought leader writes

the product and recommends it, this could be enough to change the "no see" physician's mind. If the physician starts writing the product, he or she will begin to want samples … and then I'm in!

- Gaining information from the physician's office staff about his or her main patient population and likes and dislikes.
- Consistently providing current and useful information (journal articles, recent research findings, and so on) to the physician through his or her staff.
- Asking the staff if there are any extenuating circumstances in which the physician would agree to see reps. Once I gain the support of the office staff, I'll be well on my way.
- Building on the great rapport I have with the office staff, I'll be able to determine where the physician spends the majority of his or her time. Whether it's at a hospital, a satellite clinic, or a golf course, I will try and meet the physician there."

96. Your physician continually and emphatically states that he or she has been writing a lot of prescriptions for your product. Your reports show that he hasn't written any. What do you do?

Great Answer: "Most prescribers know that reps have very good data on their writing habits. If a doctor tells me that he or she is writing, but it isn't showing up, it may be that many patients are going to pharmacies that don't report their numbers (e.g., Wal-Mart or Sam's Club). It is usually considered taboo to confront a doctor with this data, especially if it is used to contradict him or her. The quickest way to kill my relationship with any doctor is to insinuate that he or she is a liar. First, I would consult with my teammates to see if this has happened to them with the same doctor. If it has happened previously and the teammates were able to remedy the situation, I could learn from them. However, if my colleagues and I continue to experience similar reactions from this physician, it would be best to consult with our manager. Touchy situations like this call for wisdom, and what better source of wisdom than my manager?"

97. After introducing yourself to a physician, what will your next course of action be?

Great Answer: "I'll start out by asking open-ended questions about the physician and his or her practice, such as: How long have you been in practice? Where did you go to school? Where are you from? Where did you complete your residency? What has been your clinical experience with this drug? What's your first line of therapy choice for this specific patient population?

"Everyone likes to talk about themselves, and doctors are no different. I will find out what they like to do in their spare time and what their hobbies are. I might ask if they are a fan of a state school or of a specific professional sports team. Also, if I see pictures or other clues around the office that he or she is married and/or has kids, I will ask about his or her family.

"I will utilize the same questioning strategies with the rest of the office and nursing staff. The better my relationships with them, the easier it will be for me to obtain access to the physician. Each visit in the beginning should focus on gathering intelligence. The more I know about the physician, the easier it will be to extend the call, or to start the conversation in a way that engages the doctor and increases my chance of making an impact that day.

"I also plan to create a spreadsheet for each person in the office, not just the doctor. I'll enter notes about what the doctor and staff told me that day. If I don't write this valuable information down, I may forget 90 percent of it before the next visit to that office. Once I have acquired personal-interest information and really feel like I understand the physician, I will be able to zero in on his or her prescribing habits and philosophies. By utilizing questioning strategies, building trusting relationships with the physicians and office staff, and keeping track of all essential details, I will possess the valuable information necessary to plan my approach with each prescriber."

THINK TWICE WHEN SENDING A RÉSUMÉ

When e-mailing your résumé, always send two versions: one in Word or another word-processed document, and one that has been converted to ASCII. By sending two documents, you cover your bases. If the recipient is unable to open or read your Word file, he or she will be able to read your ASCII version. Be sure to mention that you have sent two versions for his or her convenience.

98. After your product presentation, the physician states that he or she is happy with your competition's product and won't consider yours. What would you do?

Great Answer: "I would start out by telling the physician that I respect his or her opinion. Then, I would probe to determine the specific criteria he or she is using to make the choice as well as the criteria for determining whether the drug is successful. For example, does he or she write based upon efficacy studies or by the percentage of patient compliance? Based upon that information, I'll know better how to position my product so that it meets and exceeds the criteria for prescribing and analyzing successful treatments."

99. A physician states that your product is more expensive than your competitor's and that's why he or she won't consider a change. What do you do next?

Great Answer: "I would tell the physician that I understand cost is a major issue, but I would also probe to determine what other factors are important to him or her when treating this specific patient population type. Based upon that information, I would be able to highlight the aspects of my product that clearly are beneficial compared to those of the competition. Also, if my drug has a more favorable price and favorable tier placement on other health care plans, I would present those specific formulary coverages. And I would ask for a commitment to try my drug with the next three patients who are on those particular (cheaper, with better tier placement) health care plans. Once the physician sees the efficacy and benefits of my product, I can incrementally move him or her closer to the goal of writing 100 percent for this specific patient population."

100. If your product and your competitor's product cost the same, how would you differentiate your product?

Your Plan: This is essentially the same as Question #99, so you can answer it in much the same way.

Great Answer: "First, I would probe to understand the specific factors that influence the physician in his or her prescribing behavior for the specific patient population. If price is one of the factors, which it usually is, I would state that I understand cost is a big issue—because respecting the physician's opinion is paramount. I would obtain knowledge of my product's formulary status in various leading health care plans, and I would highlight those plans in which my product has a favorable formulary status. I would also highlight other factors the physician noted as influencing his or her prescribing habits, showing for those factors how my product clearly has more benefits to the physician and his or her patients. For example, if the physician states that convenient, once-daily dosing is important to his or her prescribing habits, and if my product has once-daily dosing, I would highlight that particular fact.

"In addition, if I know that a physician is particularly close to a specialist or highly respects another 'thought leader' who happens to be a significant prescriber of mine, I might ask that physician to recommend me and my product as well as to speak to the success his or her patients have had with it.

"Finally, inviting the physician to a speaker program or providing a number of company-approved journal articles might provide the proof the physician needs to begin prescribing my products on a consistent basis."

101. The physician will not try your product, nor will he or she tell you why. What would you do?

Great Answer: "Probing for prescribing habits is very important. If the physician is unwilling to speak with me about that, however, I would need to focus on developing a better rapport with him or her. Presuming that I have developed good relationships with the office staff, I would utilize those relationships to build a better rapport with the doctor as well as to get a window into his or her prescribing habits. I can also discern from them the types of actions—speaker programs, journal articles, lunch and learns, referrals from respected physicians, and so on—that would most influence the physician."

STEVE, WHO WAS INTERVIEWING WITH ASTRAZENECA, OFFERED THE FOLLOWING:

"With AstraZeneca, they really emphasize the situational-type questions in the interview, and you have to answer them in the STAR format. The STAR questions took up about half of the time in the interviews that I had with the company. They are not difficult, but you must think quickly, be clear, not too verbose, and stick to the format. A question I was asked was, 'Give an example of a time when you did something at work that your boss didn't like even though you thought that you had done a good job on it. Explain what happened.'"

Can you think of a good answer for Steve?

102. **Your partner is not keeping up with his or her responsibilities, and this is affecting your relationship with physicians. What do you do?**

Great Answer: "The first thing I'd do is to have a conversation with my partner and ask if there's anything that's affecting his or her ability to do the job. Who knows … there could be health issues, family problems, or the like. If nothing is accomplished or solved within a couple of weeks, I'd be forced to speak with our manager about the issue. Obviously, I wouldn't want to lose the momentum we've gained with our doctors, and I wouldn't want my partner's conduct to reflect poorly on our company. Therefore, I'd make sure that the physicians are getting what they need and that I follow through on promises made."

103. **This job occasionally requires you to leave the field for training. How do you prepare your customers for this leave?**

Great Answer: "By letting customers know when I'll be gone and when I'll return as well as having a backup plan for their needs. I would also assure customers that I will be checking phone messages, and following up with them, while I am away. Before leaving, I'd check in with each customer personally, to make sure their sample supplies are adequately stocked and to address any questions or needs."

104. **Reps often must work a display at local medical conventions. How do you prepare, and what should you do once there?**

Great Answer: "The night before, I would attach the most influential company-provided literature pieces to the company-supplied display boards, so that they are as attractive as possible. I would arrive early in the morning to find the best location, if it had not previously been assigned, setting up displays in the area of highest traffic. I'd make sure to greet the physicians and ask open-ended questions to engage them in dialogue. I would continue the dialogue with questions that facilitate discussions about the benefits of my product to the physicians' patients and medical practices."

105. **How will you establish credibility and respect with physicians?**

Great Answer: "If I am a regular source of information important to physicians and I strive to become a product and disease-state expert, physicians may actually look forward to engaging in intelligent conversation with me! Also, if I provide as many proof sources as possible in a manner that appears objective, physicians will learn to trust what I say. Finally, if I learn physicians' prescribing habits and become a consultative partner who adds value to their practice, physicians' respect and trust will follow."

Interview Questions and GREAT Answers that Showcase Your Sales Skills (Prowess)

(Even if you haven't held a sales position, your answers here need to show that you understand the basics of selling and that you possess the skills that are required to make sales.)

106. How would you describe "selling"?

Great Answer: "Selling starts with active listening to determine a client's needs and rapport building to gain trust. Once the needs are uncovered, selling progresses to positioning products accordingly and closing for a small, specific action. Those small, specific actions will eventually lead toward the global goal of the physician's utilizing my product versus that of the competition in every applicable situation."

ARE YOU SURE THAT YOU WANT TO BE A PHARMA REP?

An average rep during an average day spends approximately 30 to 60 minutes making sales presentations. The remainder of the day is spent preparing for calls, driving to and from offices, making small talk with office staff, stocking samples, and waiting in waiting rooms.

107. What has been your greatest sales achievement?

What They're Trying to Determine: Obviously, this question is asked to uncover your priorities. Did the sales achievement generate a lot of money for you or your company? Or was the result more intangible, such as swaying opinion to take a specific course of action?

Your Plan/Great Answer: You must answer this question in STAR format and be prepared to defend why it was your greatest sales achievement. Whether the result was tangible or not, make sure to link it to some sort of tangible result. For example, you may have presented detailed, objective information that influenced the school board to "rethink" the all-day kindergarten program and revert back to half days. As a result, the district realized a 30 percent decrease in expenses, due to the elimination of full-day kindergarten classes. (See how the "intangible" became "tangible"?)

S _____

_____

T _____

_____

A _____

_____

R_____

_____

108. What are some closing strategies you might use with a physician?

A Few Great Answers:

A. "You've stated that cost and dosing schedules are important to you in prescribing medication for your diabetic patients. With the Tier II placement on Aetna health care and the once-daily dosing to increase patient compliance, will you write product X for your next five diabetic patients that have not had success with prior medications?"

B. "You've stated that cost and dosing schedules are important to you in prescribing medication for your diabetic patients. With the Tier II placement on Aetna health care, which ensures cost effectiveness, and the once-daily dosing to increase patient compliance, will you write product X for your next five new diabetic patients?"

C. "We've talked about cost and dosing schedules with product X. Will you commit to speaking with me next time about this journal article I'm leaving with you?"

D. "We've talked about cost and dosing schedules with product X, but you've stated that efficacy studies are also important in your prescribing decisions. With that being said, will you commit to attending our speaker program to learn more about those studies from our speaker, Dr. Reynolds?"

E. "You've stated that cost and dosing schedules are important to you in prescribing medication for your diabetic patients. Product X has Tier II placement on Aetna health care and once-daily dosing to increase patient compliance. Plus, you've reported that your last 10 patients on product X have had super results. With that being said, will you agree to make product X your first line of treatment for your diabetic patients?"

109. Tell me about a time when your sales method didn't work. What could you have done differently?

Your Plan/Great Answer: Make sure that the error you committed wasn't a big issue and nor was the poor result. Also, be sure to state what you did to keep the error from happening again and how your new method ensured successful results from then on. By utilizing the STAR format, your response will contain all the necessary elements for a complete answer that pleases the interviewer.

S _____

_____

T _____

_____

A _____

_____

R_____

_____

Your "new method" for keeping it from happening again: _____

_____

_____

Successful results by utilizing this new method: _____

_____

_____

110. Tell me about a time when you sold someone an idea. What was your method?

Your Plan/Great Answer: Answering in the STAR format is essential, as this is a behavioral question. It is designed to prove whether you can sell an intangible product, which is really what pharmaceutical sales is all about. Even though the products themselves are not intangible, you are not selling them on the spot and you are not having your customers sign by the X. Be sure to emphasize the method you used to sell the idea. Highlight the relationship building skills, the active listening skills, and the way you presented the information that led to your success.

S _____

_____

T _____

_____

A _____

_____

R_____

_____

111. Sell me something.

Your Plan/Great Answer: If the manager asks you to sell him or her something, consider the following points:

- If you want to make a huge impact, and you have previously conducted your research and created a product presentation binder, why not go for it? Set yourself apart from other candidates by selling one of the company's actual products. Even if your detail does not work perfectly, the manager still will give you big points for having had the guts to try it.

- You could sell his or her own company to the manager. Take information off the company's website. Most companies have a credo, key values, or mission statement with several key points that could be sold to a client.

- Sell an object or concept that you know well so that your passion and conviction shine through. Bring the item with you and keep it in your bag ... just in case.

Example: You are selling a Microsoft Optical Computer Mouse. (Bring the object with you or take a picture of it, if possible.)

1. Build rapport by asking a question that the customer would be interested in, based upon your previously gained knowledge of the customer.

2. Utilize open-ended questioning strategies that relate to your product. For example, "When you're deciding upon a computer mouse to purchase, what factors are important to you?"

3. Features and *Benefits*

   • Ribbed, clear, scrolling wheel that lights up when pressed— *ribbed design allows user to control the speed and allows for precise navigation; lighted wheel alerts that the button has been pressed and the scrolling mechanism is on.*
   Gain agreement: "Is that important to you?" Then "build a bridge" to the next feature or benefit.

   • Perfectly asymmetrical—*ergonomically comfortable for both left- and right-handed users.*
   Gain agreement again: "Is this of interest to you?" Then "build a bridge" to the next feature or benefit.

   • Customizable buttons—*allow users to assign short keyboard macros, thus saving time and repetition.*
   Gain agreement again: "Do customizable buttons matter to you when choosing your computer mouse?"

4. Summarize and close. Gain agreement from the customer to commit to a certain action, such as to try the Microsoft Optical Computer Mouse the next time he or she is considering buying a new mouse.

ROLE-PLAYING DURING AN INTERVIEW

If you make it to the final round of interviews, you can bet that you will be asked to role-play. You will need to know the basic stages of the sales call. Usually the interviewer poses as the doctor and you play the role of the rep selling to the doctor. This is an exercise that is dreaded by many candidates, especially those with limited or no sales experience. By following a basic sales call formula, however, anyone can learn to sell any product.

The key is to be familiar with the basic components of a sales call (basic is just fine for interview purposes).

Anatomy of a simple sales call:

1. **Introduce yourself.**

For example: *"Hello, Doctor Smith, it's nice to see you again. I'm Joe Smith, your Pharmacia rep. Today I would like to tell you about a new product that I think you are going to like a lot. Can I have a few minutes with you to tell you about this pen?"* Show the doctor the pen, but don't let him or her handle it.

2. **Uncover your customer's needs.**

What is he or she looking for in a pen? A pen that writes longer than any other pen? A Mont Blanc–type of pen that portrays a successful, professional image?

Discover the customer's needs, and you will then know which of the pen's features to emphasize. If you want to talk about the great felt tip and the customer could care less about the felt tip, it would be a mistake to focus your sales call on the felt tip. If you do, you will not sell any pens!

How do you uncover your customer's needs? You ask open-ended questions about them!

For example: *"Doctor, before I begin to tell you about this pen, I would like to find out about the pens that you currently use. I know that there are other pens that you use and like. What is it that makes you choose one pen over another?"*

3. **Listen.**

Listen to what the customer tells you because he or she is telling you what his or her needs are. For example, a customer might say, "I like a pen that has a nice grip, and the ink color is really important to me."

4. **Use feature-and-benefit selling to show the customer that your product meets his or her needs.**

You have uncovered the customer's needs, and you know what he or she is looking for in a pen. Show via very basic feature-and-benefit selling that your pen is one he or she will like and should use.

What is a feature?

A feature is a physical component of the pen, such as:
- felt tip
- black ink
- comfortable grip
- size
- overall look

What is a benefit?

A benefit is always connected to a particular feature and answers the question, "So what?"

For example: *"This pen has a quick-dry tip (feature). Because it has a quick-dry tip, you can rest assured that all of the prescriptions you write will be smudgeproof, eliminating calls from pharmacists who can't make out your writing (benefit)."*

The interviewer may mention more than one need. Cover each of them with feature-and-benefit selling.

5. **Close.**

Once you have demonstrated that your pen meets all of the interviewer's needs, ask him or her a question that gives him or her the opportunity to raise an objection, if there is one. If there's no objection, close and ask for the business.

For example: *"Doctor, you said that you are interested in a pen that is smudgeproof and has a nice grip. Have I shown you that this pen is smudgeproof and has a nice grip?"*

If the interviewer has an objection, listen to it and address the issue. If there is no further objection, close!

For example: *"Doctor, it sounds to me like this pen is one that you can really put to good use. Would you agree? Would you be willing to give this pen a try?"*

When the doctor agrees to try the pen, thank him or her and state that you are looking forward to coming back and getting his or her feedback.

112. What do you see as the key skills in closing?

Great Answer: "Because of the nature of this business and the fact that much of a rep's time is spent trying to develop rapport with physicians, many reps forget to close all their calls. My goal would be to close every time. I think there are many skills that are important when it comes to closing: developing rapport; employing active listening to determine customers' needs; positioning the product to meet their needs; establishing trusting/consultative relationships; utilizing trial closes throughout sales calls; and asking for a commitment to talk again, to read a particular study, or to prescribe my product for a specific patient type."

113. Describe a situation in which you were part of a team and things didn't go well. Then tell me about a situation in which you made things work in a team environment.

Your Plan/Great Answer: Obviously, the first half of this question is negative in nature and designed to make you reveal a fatal flaw. *Don't do it!* It doesn't say that the example you choose must have had a negative result … just that things did not go well. This could refer to challenges along the way, not necessarily the end result.

First Question: Not going well at first … a couple of problems … but the team obtained good results anyway

S _____
_____

T *Don't forget to mention how things were not going well or what the challenges were along the way:* _____
_____

A _____
_____

R_____
_____

Second Question: Made things work in a team environment with good results

S _____
_____

T _____
_____

A _____
_____

R_____
_____

For both questions, emphasize your rapport-building skills, listening skills, ability to create consensus among colleagues, and ability to motivate and inspire your teammates toward a common goal.

What usually is your role on a team—motivator, leader, "get it done" person, "big picture" person, or other?

Great Answer: "I think flexibility is an important characteristic of a successful team member. The very nature of a team is constantly changing based upon the different backgrounds and experiences of the team members. Because of this, it's important to take on differing roles, as necessary. One day, I may be the motivator—the one who provides positive feedback and encourages team members to keep going. The next day, I may be the leader of a specific project because I have the most expertise in the project area. And yet another day, I may be the person who takes the list of 'to do's' and gets to work without waiting for others to help. When each member of a team is flexible (ready and willing to do 'whatever it takes'), the project is accomplished with greater ease and extraordinary success!"

 THE "TRIAL CLOSE"

Pharmaceutical sales, one of the hottest markets for job seekers, requires the ability to "close". The first and most important opportunity to show potential employers how effectively you can close a deal is during the interview. A "trial close" to the interview follows the introduction and questioning period. It occurs when the candidate asks whether the interviewer approves of him or her for the job or sees hurdles to his or her getting the position. A question to ask might be: "Is that what you're looking for?"

115. What do you like least about working as a member of a team?

Great Answer: "I think there are so many great things about working as part of a team—challenging each other, learning from each other, and working toward a common goal. The only occasionally difficult thing about working as a member of a team is that there can be a mix of personalities and pre-conceived notions about doing things a certain way. This can make it difficult to achieve consensus of opinion about the steps necessary to achieve a goal. Therefore, patience, understanding, respect, flexibility, and good communication skills are imperative skills when working as part of a team."

116. How would you explain your job to a young child?

Great Answer: "I would say that I work with doctors to help them know which medications will work best for people who are sick. The reason it's so important is that when doctors know which medicines work the best, it helps people live longer and better."

The dreaded, but not so bad, situational questions.
(What the heck are they anyway?)

Situational questions usually are asked at some point in the pharmaceutical sales interview process. They usually are hypothetical in nature and are asked to see how you would respond if you were in a particular situation. Managers like to ask these questions to find out more about your character and personality.

Great Answer to a Situational Question:

117. What would you do if a doctor asked you a question that you couldn't answer?

Great Answer: "I would acknowledge that I didn't know the answer and would try, while still in the doctor's office, to find an answer. Perhaps referring to the product's package insert would help me out, or I might have the answer with me in my documentation. If I couldn't find the answer while still there, I would make it a priority to find the answer and to get back to the doctor within 24 hours. Returning to his or her office the next day with an answer to the question would actually be a great excuse for a follow-up call. The last thing I would want to do is attempt to answer a question that I actually didn't know the answer to. I'm building a relationship in that office and have a reputation to protect. I don't want to ruin my credibility by answering incorrectly. I think it is reasonable to believe that customers don't expect us to know everything and that they respect us when we admit that we can't answer correctly at that given moment."

The Pharmaceutical Sales Interview Process: Step by Step

Just about all pharmaceutical sales interviews start with a phone interview. Most of the time, your interview will end and you still won't know if you have made the cut for the next interview, the face-to-face. You can ask for a face-to-face during the phone interview, but don't expect to get one on the spot.

The first face-to-face interview is usually with the district manager. Depending on the manager, you may be one of thirty or one of three being interviewed. Some managers love to interview; others prefer to keep the candidate list to a minimum. Always ask for another interview when the first face-to-face is over, but again—don't expect to get one right then and there.

A manager will often offer a second round of face-to-face interviews to condense the candidate list. This interview can occur up two months after the initial phone interview. Managers often travel a lot, and there can be lag time between interviews. If there does turn out to be lag time, be sure to keep in touch with the interviewing manager during the interim. You don't want him or her to forget about you, plus you want to show your continued interest in the position.

The next step is usually a "ride with" (spending a day in the field with one of the star reps in the district). At this point, the field has usually been narrowed to one or two other candidates. Keep in mind that the rep you are riding with will be reporting back with blow-by-blow details of your day together, so be on your best behavior. (Refer to the tips below.)

Usually, the final step in the interview process is another meeting with the district manager, this time also with the regional manager. This interview is usually a formality to get the stamp of approval from the regional manager. Unless you really goof up, you usually have the job in the bag. An offer may or may not come during the interview. Sometimes the offer is contingent upon passing drug and background checks.

TIPS FOR A "RIDE WITH" DAY, ALSO KNOWN AS A "PRECEPTORSHIP"

- Smile a lot.
- Make a new friend!
- Dress your best (conservative dark suit).
- Don't badmouth your current boss.
- Be positive and enthusiastic.
- Interact with the office staff when appropriate—say hello, engage in small talk, and so on, but don't overdo it. You don't want to be a distraction from what the rep is there to do.
- Don't ask questions like "What time do you cut out of here on Friday afternoons?"
- Do ask some questions about the district manager. The rep may be able to give you ideas about what it will take to make the final cut. Find out what the manager is looking for and who the competition is.
- Relax, be yourself, and have fun! Get as much out of the experience as you can, and add this preceptorship to your résumé as soon as you get back home.
- Thank the rep in writing for his or her time and information, sending the note as soon as possible after the ride with.

The Phone Interview

The phone interview may be your most difficult interview because you will usually have a short amount of time to make a good impression. You also don't have the advantage of meeting the interviewer in person. Sorry, but your good eye contact will not help over the phone!

With phone interviews, *the best personality wins.* If you got the call, you have what it takes on paper. The caller is now in the screening process and wants to find out if you can hold a conversation with someone. The caller is also looking for energy and enthusiasm, so let it show in your voice. Be prepared to answer questions and to let your personality shine. Have fun, and relax!

Be sure to ask for a face-to-face interview before hanging up, and save the caller's phone number for follow-up.

There are so many pharmaceutical companies that it is difficult to predict what questions may be asked during a phone interview. In some instances, the manager is not the one who makes the phone call—sometimes, human resources personnel make the call (often the case if a company is going through a major expansion). As a rule, however, you can expect to be asked questions intended to screen out candidates and to save the manager precious time.

Screening questions that you may be asked during the phone interview.

(Refer to the Great Answers section of the book
for specifics on how to answer.)

Why are you looking for a pharmaceutical sales position?

The caller is making sure you have a good idea of what the job entails and that you are interested in pharmaceutical sales specifically. If you answer that any sales job will do, you may lose your chance to continue on in the interview process. Managers want to hire people who are eager for pharmaceutical sales and only pharmaceutical sales.

What is your salary at your current job?

Surprisingly, this is the question that eliminates the majority of candidates over the phone. If you are making a substantial salary now and are willing to take a pay cut to pursue a pharmaceutical sales career, most managers, especially those in human resources, won't allow you to continue on in the interview process.

Many applicants have the misperception that they can start out with a poorly performing territory and turn it into a big commission earner in no time. The reality is that it takes time to turn a territory around. Sometimes it can take up to a year to see the results of hard work. Relationships have to be built with customers—and relationship building takes time. Most managers prefer to hire someone with a salary that is comparable to what they have to offer. It makes good business sense.

Suggestion: If you are making a good salary in your current position and you are asked what you are earning, give only your base salary information. Tell the manager that you are well aware of what pharmaceutical reps make and that you are prepared to work for a similar salary. (Starting salaries in pharmaceutical sales range from $40K–$60K plus commissions and/or bonuses. Some companies offer higher salaries in lieu of large commissions. Most companies pay quarterly commissions; some offer an end-of-year bonus.)

Are you available for overnight travel?

If you want to work as a pharmaceutical representative, no matter what the company, some overnight travel will be required. Smaller, more urban territories usually require very little overnight travel. Regardless of the geography of the territory, be prepared to spend some overnights in hotels for district meetings, regional sales meetings, national sales meetings, and sales training programs. Meetings are usually two to three nights in duration—usually quarterly. Initial training can involve several weeks at a time at the corporate headquarters.

Are you interviewing with any other companies?

I have gotten several emails from candidates verifying that this question was asked during their phone interview and inquiring how they should have answered the question. (Refer to the Great Answers section for the best way to answer.)

ACTUAL PHONE INTERVIEW STORY
Carla, who interviewed with Innovex,
offered the following:

"My phone interview was with a person from an outside company who was hired to do the phone screening. The woman sounded like she had just interviewed about 100 people. She was very matter of fact and to the point ... almost as if she couldn't wait for the day to end. Needless to say, it was tough to get a conversation going with her. She told me I had 20 minutes to answer six situational questions and that she would be taking notes by hand. One of the questions I was asked was: 'What would you do if you encountered a doctor who was annoyed that you were in his office because your counterpart had been in just 10 minutes earlier promoting the same products?'"

Doing your homework

(*Hint:* Do it *before* the phone interview!)

Research the company.

Make no mistake about it: the more you know about a company and its products, the more you will impress the interviewer and the better you will do overall. Before your interview, you must do a comprehensive company and industry search. Start out on a company's website and gather information about its products and financials, and employment in general. Many of the websites have direct links to product advertisements. Use this consumer-friendly information to get the basics. Don't bog yourself down with product details. A couple of features and benefits should be all that you need for initial interviews. If you don't do your research, you will appear unmotivated to work for the company. In other words, if you haven't done your homework, don't bother going to the interview.

The following are some useful sites for additional research:

- **Hoovers Online:** (*www.hoovers.com*) Company and industry profiles
- **Bloomberg:** (*www.bloombergs.com*) Industry and market data
- **Edgar Database:** (*www.edgar-online.com*) Electronic data gathering, analysis, and retrieval system
- **Morning Star:** (*www.morningstar.com*) Stock information
- **Web100:** (*www.w100.com*) Largest American and global companies based on revenue
- **Thomas Regional:** (*www.thomasregional.com*) Company research by product and industry
- **Working Mother Magazine** (*www.workingmother.com*): 100 best companies for working mothers
- **Employers of choice 500:** (*www.employersofchoice.com*) From BestJobsUSA.com
- **Web MD** (*www.webmd.com*) Consumer friendly information about diseases, drugs, and so on
- **Rx List** (*www.rxlist.com*) Prescribing information for most drugs that are approved in the United States

What you need to know:

- Corporate headquarters location(s)
- Products—a basic knowledge of what you will be promoting
- Who the company's customers are (family practitioners, pulmonologists, ENTs, and so on)
- History
- Recent news
- Competitors (You won't need to know too many details. A few product brand names will be plenty.)
- Financial news

Tip: Bring a copy of the information you have compiled about the company to the interview. Managers will be impressed that you are well prepared. If you really want to impress your interviewer, bring along some copies of the company's current journal advertisements. Find them in the *New England Journal of Medicine* and the *Journal of the American Medical Association (JAMA).* As well as impressing the managers by having this information in hand, you will also be better prepared for your interview. By looking at their journal ads, you will know which products they are currently promoting and you will also see, in print, their marketing messages.

Before the Interview

- Practice, practice, practice answers to common and more difficult questions.
- Prepare a list of questions to ask.

- Gather several copies of your résumé, a list of references, and a professional-looking brag book (refer to the information about brag books in this guidebook).
- Dress your absolute best.
- Dress conservatively (dark blue is always a good choice of color).
- Bring a pen and notepad to jot down information after the interview—but don't take notes during the interview.

During the Interview

(When all is said and done, the best personality wins!)

- *You must be energetic, friendly, and enthusiastic!* This is the most important tip in this section. If you are not enthusiastic, no matter how well you answer the questions, you will not land the job. Enthusiasm sells!
- Shake hands firmly.
- Make eye contact.
- Establish rapport.
- Make a friend. (Your interviewer wants to find out if you are someone he or she will enjoy working with.)
- Laugh and smile (when appropriate).
- Be a good listener.
- Convey your drive and dedication.
- Don't lie.
- Don't say anything negative about a previous employer.
- Don't ask salary questions during the first interview.
- Be yourself. Have fun, and relax!

Smart Questions to Ask Your Interviewer.

(You're only half prepared for your interview
if you plan only to answer questions!)

Every great interviewee should go to an interview prepared to ask questions as well as to answer them. Your goal, when asked if you have any questions, is to show genuine interest in the company, the job, and the interviewer. Having nothing to ask makes you appear passive and not interested in the position. Go prepared to ask a few smart questions, and avoid looking like a deer in the headlights.

1. Ask about the competitive environment as well as the goals of the organization and management.
2. Ask what skills the interviewer considers to be most important for the position.
3. Ask the interviewer if he or she sees a gap in your skills. If a gap is identified, this gives you an opportunity to identify skills you possess that you haven't already talked about in the interview.
4. Ask again about a gap in your skills. If the answer is no, close, and ask for the next interview. Managers always like interviewees to ask for another interview. Closing is what sales is all about! Good closers make excellent salespeople.

Additional information you might like to gather from your interviewer:

- Detailed description of position (if you don't already know).
- Reason position is available.
- Territory status and history.
- Anticipated training program.

- Realistic earnings potential of successful salespeople. (Don't bring this up in your first interview.)
- Company growth plans, market share, and competitors.
- Why and when did the interviewer join the company?

Important: Don't forget to ask for the interviewer's card and e-mail address, and follow up immediately with a thank-you note.

Breaking the Ice:

The key to starting your interview out well is to break the ice. Having some good icebreaker questions to ask helps you make a good first impression and sets the tone for the interview. Small talk gives the interviewer an opportunity to get a feel for your personality and also gives you an idea of his or her personality. Most importantly, it gives you time to become acquainted and to ease any tension and anxiety you may be feeling as you begin the interview. Furthermore, taking the time to break the ice is important because it is a skill you will use all the time when presenting to doctors. By showing your interviewer that you are good at breaking the ice, they will be able to envision you doing the same as you call on doctors. Be sure to ask only questions that the interviewer will be happy to answer, and *don't ask all of them.* Select those you feel are the most appropriate for your situation, and ask only as many as you see fit. You do want to get on to the interview, after all.

Some samples of ice breakers:

- What is your position at the company (if you don't know)?
- How long have you been with the company?
- How long are you in town?

- Have you had a chance to get out to any good restaurants or to see any of the sites (if the interviewer is from out of town)?
- What do you think about this weather?
- What an easy trip. The directions were great! (Be positive. If you got lost for an hour and thought that the directions were horrific, don't say so! Remember, you are behaving like the sales rep of the century. Smile at all times, regardless of how you really feel.)

Relax During the Interview. Be Yourself.

When interviewing for pharmaceutical sales positions, you want the interview to be as conversational as possible. One of your main goals while interviewing is to "be yourself". You want to answer questions in a way that displays your enthusiasm for the job, your belief in yourself, and your confidence about what you can offer the company.

The job candidate who is chosen isn't necessarily the one with the most experience. In sales, the interviewee with the best personality usually lands the job. You want your personality to shine through during the interview: Relax, and keep in mind that the person doing the interviewing was probably in your shoes not so long ago. Think of the interviewer as your peer, someone you are having a conversation with. If you relax and believe in yourself, you will present yourself as the best candidate for the job. With persistence, determination, and a little practice, almost anyone can learn to interview with confidence and composure.

Come up with a general idea of how you might answer the common questions asked in virtually all interviews. Practice your answers, but don't memorize them. Don't be afraid to take a minute before answering to gather your thoughts. A well-thought-out answer is better than an off-the-cuff one. Take the time, a day or two before the interview, to mentally review your accomplishments and the high points of your résumé. You should be able to rattle off your qualifications, your academic credentials, and your successful career experiences as effortlessly as reciting your name and phone number. There are literally hundreds of interview questions that can be asked in an interview. It's impossible and unrealistic to attempt to practice answers to all of them. If you get caught up in memorizing answers to questions, you will be doing yourself a disservice. Memorized answers sound canned and unnatural.

Common Interview Questions

In this book, we have outlined some of the most common questions asked in pharmaceutical sales interviews. That compilation of questions is by no means comprehensive. Go to your interview prepared to answer the following general most common questions as well. Study up!

- What are your strengths?
- Tell me about your last positions. Which ones did you enjoy the most? the least?
- Are you happy with your career's progress to date?
- Tell me about yourself.
- What do you expect to get out of your career?
- What is the most difficult situation you have ever faced?
- How do you define "success"?
- What were the three most important events (positive or negative) in your life?
- What do you consider your most significant accomplishment?
- What is your favorite book?

- What do you like and dislike about presentations, and why?
- Tell me about your last day at work.
- What are the things that motivate you?
- If money was no object and you wanted to work, what would be your ideal position?
- What are your foreign language capabilities?
- What jobs have you enjoyed the most and the least, and why?
- What can you offer us that someone else can't?
- Tell me about your education. Do you have plans for further education?
- How has your schooling prepared you for this job?
- How would your current supervisor describe you?
- What are your primary activities outside of work?
- How do you handle people that you don't get along with?
- What makes you think you can handle this position?
- What has been your greatest challenge?
- What do you look for in a job?
- What three adjectives would you say best describe you?

Questions Asked of Recent College Graduates

- What is your GPA? Do you feel it reflects your abilities?
- How has your educational experience prepared you for this position?
- What was your favorite course in college, and why?
- Why did you decide to attend X College? Are you happy with your choice?
- What factors did you consider in choosing your major?
- How did your college experience change you?

Crucial Closing Questions That You
Should Ask Your Interviewer

*Asking these questions will help you advance to the next step
in the interview process.*

1. What additional information do you need regarding my candidacy?
2. Can you please explain the rest of the interview process? Where do I go from here?
3. Is there anything that is preventing me from continuing on in the interview process?
4. How do I compare to my competition?
5. Can we set up the next interview now?

Thank You Letter

Your Name
Address
City, State, ZIP
Phone
E-mail address
Date of interview

Date

Mr./Ms. Manager Name
Title
Address
City, State, ZIP

Dear Mr./Ms. Manager,

It was a pleasure meeting with you earlier today. I enjoyed learning more about ABC Pharmaceuticals.

I hope that I conveyed to you how excited I am about the prospect of working for you. My internships and part-time jobs in medical areas have given me a clear idea of what a pharmaceutical sales career would entail. I truly feel a calling to this type of work.*

I know that you expect the search to last a few more weeks. In the meantime, please don't hesitate to call me if you need further information.

Many thanks for your consideration. I am looking forward to hearing from you.

Sincerely,
(*signature*)

Your Name

* *You may also want to add a sentence or two about something specific that was discussed during the interview.*

Be sure to send this immediately following the interview.

Resignation Letter

Your Name
Address
City, State, ZIP
Phone
E-mail address

Date

Name
Company
Street Address
City, State, Zip

Dear _____:

Please accept this letter as my formal resignation from my position with *(name of company)*. I have accepted a position as *(job title)* with *(name of company)*, and my last date of employment will be *(date)*.

Although I have enjoyed working with you and my coworkers at *(name of employer)*, I feel I could not pass up this opportunity to take my career in a new and exciting direction.

In closing, I would like to express my deep gratitude for the training and guidance you have given me over the years. I will always be appreciative.

Sincerely,
(signature)

Your name

Pharmaceutical Sales Websites:

www.pharmaceuticalsalesinterviews.com (Lisa's website)

www.pharmaceutical-rep.com (Anne's website)

www.pharmadiversity.com

www.coreynahman.com

www.biospace.com

www.cafepharma.com

www.hirerx.com

www.medzilla.com

www.pharmaceuticaljobsusa.com

www.pharmaopportunities.com

www.rxcareercenter.com

Diversity Websites:

www.pharmadiversity.com

www.latpro.com

www.hirediversity.com

About the Authors

Anne Posegate

Anne has a B.S. in Sociology and Education and has enjoyed careers in human resource management, public relations, education, and pharmaceutical sales recruiting/corporate training.

Since 2001, Anne has committed herself to training others into their dream careers. As a master résumé writer, Anne creates powerful, attention-gaining résumés that reflect her in-depth knowledge of the pharmaceutical sales industry. As a Certified Employment Interview Coach, Anne's interview methodology focuses on empowering clients to market their unique skills and talents effectively as well as to learn and implement innovative interview strategies that have been proven to impress hiring managers and win jobs.

Building on her pharmaceutical sales recruiting experience, Anne created a pharmaceutical sales career website, *www.pharmaceutical-rep.com*, dedicated to being an information source for aspiring pharma reps. To that end, she has written and marketed a 236-page e-book system, *30 Days to Your First Pharmaceutical Sales Job,* and continues to serve as the résumé-writing and interview-coaching expert for *pharmaceutical-rep.com*—working with clients from California to Australia.

Lisa Lane

 Lisa Lane is the pharmaceutical sales industry's most visible author and consultant. She is currently president of Drug Careers, Inc., a leading pharmaceutical sales career development company that provides curricula for entry-level training programs in university programs across the United States. She is recognized as an authority in her field and is the recipient of a Marketing Destiny Award for creative sales programs. She has worked for three pharmaceutical companies in sales, product marketing, and sales training.

Lisa has served as a career expert for many pharmaceutical career websites and the career sections of many newspapers and periodicals including *"Career Builder," Sales and Marketing* magazine, the *LA Times,* the *Baltimore Sun,* the *Miami Herald,* the *Chicago Tribune,* and over 20 others. She maintains daily contact with professionals in all areas of pharmaceutical sales, counsels her customers, and devotes much of her time to staying current on pharmaceutical news and information. Since 1999, she has helped thousands break into pharmaceutical sales.

Lisa's website is *www.PharmaceuticalSalesInterviews.com.*

INDEX